ATLAS

OF

unusual

wines

PIERRICK BOURGAULT

T0283059

JONGLEZ PUBLISHING

Contents

Quebec's ice wines..7

Underwater wine...11

Orange wine..15

Wine of Montmartre..19

A monovarietal Bordeaux..25

A vine classified as a historic monument...27

Vineyard horses..31

Vineyard of the Coulée de Serrant..35

Bordeaux made with dry ice...39

Pink champagne: a very rare exception to rosé regulations..................................43

Yellow wine..49

The wine of the Padirac Cave...53

Le Clos Cristal..57

Charbonnay..61

New Year's Eve harvests..65

Night harvest at Champagne Grémillet..69

The oldest vine in the world...73

Friedrich Becker estate..75

Warrior vines..77

The walled vines of the Azores...81

Wines of Lanzarote..83

Wines of Pompeii..87

Wines of the Venetian lagoon..91

Il vino della pace: a 'peace wine' blended from 600 varieties from the five continents..........95

Sinefinis: a political wine..99

Vineyard music..101

The *alberello* vines of Pantelleria..107

Jack and the beanstalk vines..111

The strongest wine in the world..115

A sparkling wine to disgorge at home......................................119

The vineyard of pencils..123

Fuori Marmo..123

Verjuice..125

A sparkling wine to disgorge at home......................................129

Greek rosé from the Rouvalis estate..133

The amphora wines of Georgia...137

Iraq's clandestine wines...141

Wines of the Gobi desert (China)..145

Taiwan's double harvests...149

Arctic Circle

Alaska
(USA)   Fairbanks
                  o

Anchorage
   o

                                    Churchill o

                        CANADA

                                Ontario

                    o Calgary   *Rainy*
          Vancouver   Winnipeg o   *River*
                    o   **Quebec**
             o Seattle   ⊚
                                    Minnesota   Montréal o

                                                    Toronto o
                                        Chicago o
          UNITED STATES OF AMERICA
                                                        o New York

                        MEXICO

1 000 km

Quebec's ice wines

Intrepid winemakers succeed in this glacial climate

Since the discovery of the territory by French explorer Jacques Cartier in 1534, viticulture in Quebec has experienced many setbacks. Although Montreal is at the same latitude as the Bordeaux vineyards and Quebec is on a level with Burgundy, the climatic conditions are harsher. Winter kills the vine stocks if they aren't protected, frosts threaten the spring buds, the too-short summer makes it difficult for the vine to complete its growth cycle and the autumn snow follows close behind the grape pickers.

The first rootstock imported for communion wine froze, and when the vines did survive the grapes failed to ripen. In the late 19th century, some growers were planting hardier varieties. Quebec escaped a total alcohol ban in the Prohibition era, but cheap imports competed with local production and after 1930 there were no vineyards left. After four centuries of failure, it seemed an impossible dream, just as Cartier was convinced he'd found gold and diamonds in Asia when in fact he'd taken on board the pyrite and quartz of North America.

But winemakers love a challenge. Planting resumed around 1980 with grape varieties suited to the climate such as Seyval, Vidal, Geisenheim, Cayuga, Éona (whites) and Maréchal Foch, Sainte-Croix, Chaunac, Chancellor (reds).

© Luc Villeneuve

As vigorous as they were fast-growing, these varieties managed to complete their growth cycle in record time. To withstand the cold of winter, the stems are banked up (covered with a pile of soil in early November, which is removed in late April or early May) using a tractor and special tools. The growers have the most incredible equipment: burners to warm the vines, fans to combat the spring frosts, helicopters to push warm air towards the ground. Snow cannons have even been used to provide a white coat protecting the ground from the polar temperatures.

Most amazing of all, though, is the ice wine made from a grape harvest in December or January at temperatures of –8 °C to –12 °C. As water freezes at 0 °C, the ice crystals remain in the press which is kept at –7 °C: a phenomenon known as cryoselection. The concentrated juice extracted is higher in sugars and acidity and hence in aroma than it would be if the grapes were harvested and pressed at warmer temperatures. Quebec therefore respects the International Organisation of Vine and Wine rules on true ice wine.

Although 100 kilos of grapes normally yield 80–85 litres of juice, the volume is only 12–15 litres in these extreme temperatures. Working in freezing conditions for such a small yield means that ice wine is an exclusive and expensive speciality: a 0.20 litre bottle sells for around €20. Tasting reveals aromas of apricot, mango, honey and candied fruit, with a lovely fresh finish.

Quebec and Ontario are the world's largest producers. In Germany, Austria and Alsace, a handful of winegrowers also make ice wine in line with OIV standards in conditions of natural frost... This peculiar practice will become more and more rare as a result of global warming.

© Luc Villeneuve

Saint-Malo

Saint-Jean-de-Luz

FRANCE

Goriška Brda

SLOVENIA

N

500 km

Underwater wine

What happens when bottles or tanks are submerged?

From time to time, divers find old merchant ships loaded with bottles, a hundred years after they've sunk. These surviving bottles fetch high prices at auction. Are they drinkable? How does the wine react to the special conditions of the watery depths?

The low temperature slows biological changes, whereas the currents that disturb the bottles accelerate changes. Several experiments have studied the effect of the marine environment: the Drappier champagne house left 660 bottles of *Brut nature* and *Grande Sendrée 2005* for a year in the Gulf of Saint-Malo, at a temperature of 9 °C and 17 metres down in the darkness. In 2009, the Slovenian cooperative Goriška Brda also immersed crates of bottles in a freshwater stream for several years (klet-brda.si). Yannick Heude, wine merchant and president of the 'Immersion' association, studies the evolution of wines in the marine environment: 'Immersed champagne turns a darker, yellower colour, with a less lively effervescence, which would seem to support the idea that the ageing process is speeded up.'

In the bay of Saint-Jean-de-Luz (south-west France), winemaker Emmanuel Poirmeur (facebook.com/emmanuel.poirmeur) will try anything when experimenting with ageing wine; he ferments it in submerged plastic vats, with the involvement of Basque fishermen: 'What interests me is the behaviour of yeast in these conditions. In the old days, winemakers took account of the weather and the atmospheric pressure, which can vary by a factor of ten underwater, because of the tides. The temperature is 10–13 °C in winter, 17 °C in summer. So I use the ocean as an energy resource that supplies the temperature, thermal inertia, movement and counter-pressure required to make sparkling wines that it would be impossible for me to recreate ashore. I patented the method in 2007 and someone is writing a thesis on it at Montpellier University.

I'd like to pay tribute to a pioneer in this field, Jean-Louis Saget, who left some bottles of wine in oyster beds in the 1990s.' So Poirmeur prepares 500-litre leakproof, gas-porous 'Flextanks' in polyethylene, to which he adds sugar and yeast, as in a second fermentation of champagne. Divers tow them out and attach them underwater. He is making two wines, one 100 per cent maritime and the other blended with 10 per cent of the underwater wine: '10 per cent, that's enough to change the flavours. I blend, just as with barrels. I notice that the wines are fruitier, with notes of lemon, lime and yuzu.'

FRANCE

SLOVENIA

CROATIA

N

500 km

14

Orange wine

Fermenting white like red, together with their skins, to make 'orange wine'

Traditionally, white wine is made by pressing grapes (white or red) and fermenting the juice. For red wine it's the other way round: first ferment the grapes (red, of course) and then press them. In this way the tannins from the seeds, the colours and the aromas of the skins pass into the must, which in due course vinifies.

A few winemakers use the second method with white grapes. The resulting wine is still classified as white, but it has a deeper colour and more intense flavour and complexity, thanks to the presence of seeds and skins. It's known as 'macerated white', 'Italian-style' or 'orange' wine – not to be confused with the drink made from orange peel soaked in white wine with added alcohol.

Slovenian winemaker Ales Kristančič makes his *Lunar* wine in this way. Destemmed Rebula grapes are piled into Burgundy barrels to macerate, skins on. Their weight bursts the skins and sets off fermentation, a process that lasts six months. The barrels are sealed, leaving an aperture that lets carbon dioxide escape. Kristančič doesn't press these grapes, he just siphons off the juice and bottles it (on the night of the full moon). Of course, this method barely yields 25 per cent of what he'd get from pressing the contents of the barrels, but the bottled wine sells at a high price. 'A great wine is one that has taken a few risks,' says the media-savvy winemaker, who exports 80 per cent of his production and is the winner of several international awards.

In Croatia, Giorgio Clai uses the same red Burgundy method of fermentation in open barrels, although nobody from that part of France would do so with white grapes. After destemming, the grapes are macerated for thirty days and then, unlike Kristančič, Clai uses a press. 'I treat red and white in the same way, along with their skins. The first year, we destemmed by hand and pressed by foot, hence the name of the wine: *Ottocento*, as in the 1800s!'

The alcohol level is high: 'My white is the weakest at 15 per cent. My wines aren't afraid of food – it's rather food that's scared of them! This isn't really a wine for everyday drinking,' the organic grower jokes mischievously. 'I don't add sugar or yeast – I like to recognise the year and the terroir in the taste, which will vary depending on whether it rained or not.'

In France, more and more estates are making their own 'orange wine', including Gérard Bertrand in the Languedoc region. In Touraine, near Azay-le-Rideau, Marie Thibault-Cabrit produces her *Vino bianco* vintage from 100 per cent Sauvignon Blanc grapes that have been macerated for several months with their skins, 'Italian-style', in used oak barrels. She doesn't add yeast to control the fermentation or sugar to raise the level of alcohol that the grapes would naturally yield (i.e. no chaptalisation). She doesn't use much sulphite either. In the vineyard organic treatments are used with no weedkillers, and harvesting is done by hand.

Marie Thibault-Cabrit

UNITED-KINGDOM

NETHERLAND

BELGIUM

GERMANY

Lille

Amiens

LUX.

Cherbourg

Reims

Metz

Paris

Nancy

Strasbourg

Brest

Rennes

Orléans

Belfort

Dijon

Besançon

SWITZERLAND

Nantes

Poitiers

FRANCE

Clermont-
Ferrand

Limoges

Lyon

ITALY

Bordeaux

Nice

MONACO

Toulouse

Montpellier

Marseille

Perpignan

Ajaccio

SPAIN

N

100 km

Wine of Montmartre

City-centre wine reminder of a time when Île-de-France was the country's largest and most prosperous wine-producing region

Around the 2nd and 3rd centuries AD, the Parisii were so fond of the wines of Italy and southern Gaul that they planted vines in their good city of Lutetia. It's true that the grapes didn't ripen properly in the local climate but the slightly acidic flavours were greatly appreciated and the calcareous soil turned out to be suitable for a vineyard. The royal city was rich and workshops making amphorae and winepresses proliferated, as archaeological digs have revealed. Around the Parisian abbeys the monks planted vines, harvested grapes and made wine with the same enthusiasm as they did in Burgundy.

Alain Valentin, the great troubadour of the Commanderie de Montmartre, tells the story of this *king of wines and wine of kings*: 'That of the Goutte d'Or was the favourite of King Louis IX (better known as Saint-Louis, 1214–1270). On every anniversary of the royal coronation, the City of Paris was in the habit of offering four *muids** of this precious nectar to the palace.' In the 18th century, over 40,000 hectares of vines fuelled the unquenchable thirst of a prosperous and densely populated region.

But as quality doesn't necessarily go with quantity, the high yields of unripe grapes gave an acidic wine known as *guinguet* (etymology unknown) 'that could make goats dance, but people lapped it up', continues Valentin. With its low alcohol content, guinguet didn't keep well and would turn to vinegar if not quickly drunk in the *guinguettes*, the ubiquitous popular cabaret and dance halls.

* *In Paris a* muid *was equivalent to 268,220 litres (8 cubic feet).*

In the 19th century the railways brought better-quality, cheaper wines from the south of France, the expansion of Paris increased the cost of land, phylloxera killed off the rootstock and during the First World War the winemakers were slaughtered too. In the space of half a century, 2,000 years of local production were snuffed out.

In 1933, however, the City of Paris planted the tiny vineyard of Montmartre because the resident artists had objected to a building project in a garden on the northern slopes of the hill. So a vine grew in memory of those that had covered the sunnier southern slopes. Traditional harvests and vintages were sponsored by well-known artists: Mistinguett, Fernandel, Annie Cordy, Maxime Le Forestier, Pierre Perret, Gérard Jugnot, Laurent Voulzy, Nagui, Hélène Ségara, Anne Roumanoff …

Growing among the 1,800 almost exclusively red grapes (75 per cent Gamay, 20 per cent Pinot Noir, Seibel and Merlot) are a few Sauvignon Blanc, Gewurztraminer and Riesling varieties. The 18th arrondissement town hall is the only one in France whose cellar contains a bottling plant. Declaration of harvesting and bottling, tax paid, all above board.

Le Clos Montmartre is now sold during the harvest festival and throughout the year at the Musée de Montmartre (12, rue Cortot, 75018 Paris). Some old bottles are 'undrinkable', as the Festival Committee website announces with commendable frankness. Since a winemaker has become involved, however, the quality has improved significantly.

Festive harvesting of grapes from the two vines of *Chez Mélac* bistrot, Paris 11th arrondissement

The return of the Ile de France wine

Today, vines are making a comeback in Paris and a number of other towns in the surrounding Île-de-France region. Parks along with public and private gardens are embracing this very human plant which is cared for by municipal gardeners and volunteers working in associations. They prune the vines, harvest the grapes and try their hand at so-called 'garage' winemaking, wine produced in small quantities and of high quality, from a small area of vines, cultivated like a garden. For a long time, the two vines at the Mélac bistro in the 11th arrondissement of Paris were picked amid great festivities during a street party and trodden by children's feet to produce around thirty bottles of Château Charonne, which were offered in a raffle. After a period of legal uncertainty – producing alcohol remains an administrative headache – during which some vineyards were uprooted and bottles were destroyed by customs, the Vignerons Réunis Franciliens, the association of winegrowers of the region, chaired by Patrice Bersac and others, managed to obtain planting rights for the Île-de-France region, and even a protected geographical indication. In 2015, the three partners of Winerie Parisienne set up a professional urban winery in Paris and then in Montreuil, to vinify grapes purchased from different regions. In Davron, in the plains of Versailles, the three partners planted chardonnay, chenin, pinot noir and merlot. Spanning some 27 hectares, the Domaine de la Bouche du Roi is the largest in the region. Local farmers are joining them, keen to anticipate global warming. In 2019, the first harvest from a plot of Merlot will be vinified in a winery installed on the first floor of the Eiffel Tower: 'We want to put Paris back on the map of wine-producing regions and develop the future of Parisian wine, thanks in particular to tourism, which represents a source of income and a way of putting us on the map'. The temporary winery was dismantled after two and a half years, but La Bouche du Roi kept a few bottles of this first Eiffel Tower vintage – a powerful symbol of the revival of Paris wine.

Nets protecting Pierre Facon's vines from birds,
at Neuilly-Plaisance

UNITED-KINGDOM

NETHERLAND

BELGIUM

GERMANY

Lille o

Amiens o

LUX.

Cherbourg
o

Reims o

Metz o

Nancy o

Strasbourg o

Paris
■

Brest
o

Rennes
o

Orléans
o

Belfort o

Dijon o

Besançon
o

SWITZERLAND

Nantes
o

Poitiers o

FRANCE

Limoges
o

Clermont-
Ferrand
o

Lyon o

ITALY

 Bayas
o

Bordeaux o

Nice
o MONACO

Toulouse o

Montpellier
o

Marseille o

Perpignan o

Ajaccio o

SPAIN

N

100 km

A monovarietal Bordeaux

Rare example of Bordeaux wine made from a single grape variety in a world where blending different varieties is the norm

Just as an orchestra brings together several instruments, a perfumer blends different fragrances and a painter chooses a range of colours from his palette, the Bordeaux cellar masters are conductors, perfumers and artists. To make a red Bordeaux, they blend grape varieties that are authorised in the appellation zone: Merlot, Cabernet Sauvignon, Cabernet Franc and Malbec, plus a few rarities known as Petit Verdot, Villard Noir, Carménère and Fer Servadou. The first three account for 99 per cent of red grape plantations.

Each variety is harvested at maturity and the grapes are fermented in separate vats. After careful consideration and testing, the final selection of varieties is blended during an operation called assemblage, each vat lending its qualities to the desired balance of the finished wine. Watch your language here: the words *mélange* (mixture) and *coupage* (cut) are pejorative and imply mediocre wines, whereas *assemblage* is nobler.

Even in the appellations where a single variety is used – Pinot Noir in Burgundy, Gamay in Beaujolais – the plots within a holding are fermented separately, according to their maturity (which is linked to the climate and *terroir*), and are usually blended by the winegrowers. The quality of the ingredients is reflected in the finished product.

In the Bordeaux region of France, this tradition of blending different varieties dates back to the time when white and red grapes were pressed together to obtain *clairet* (claret) that was exported by ship to England and other northern countries. Growers know that it's best 'not to put all your eggs in one basket' and to cultivate varieties with different flowering times and susceptibilities, thus reducing the risks associated with heavy rainfall or disease.

After the phylloxera disaster at the end of the 19th century, the Carménère grape seemed to be extinct. In 1991, however, a root was found in Chile. Although this low-yielding variety is sensitive to *coulure* (poor fruit set when rain washes away the pollen), a few Bordeaux winegrowers replanted it anyway.

Today, with his *Pure Carménère*, Henri Duporge turns his back on the idea of blending. The wine is a monovarietal (from a single grape variety) with low yields (20 hectolitres per hectare), produced organically and free from chemicals.

Similarly, Château Belle-Vue (southern Médoc) produces a single-varietal Bordeaux wine, 100% Petit Verdot.

In 2021, the French National Institute for Origin and Quality (INAO) authorised four new grape varieties that ripen later to combat global warming: arinarnoa, castets, marselan and touriga nacional. They are intended to complement blends and maintain the style of Bordeaux, not to constitute a single-varietal wine.

UNITED-KINGDOM

NETHERLAND

BELGIUM

GERMANY

Lille ○

○ Amiens

LUX.

Cherbourg
○

○ Reims

○ Metz

Paris
■

Nancy ○

Strasbourg ○

Brest
○

Rennes
○

Orléans
○

Belfort ○

Dijon ○

Besançon
○

SWITZERLAND

Nantes
○

Poitiers ○

FRANCE

Clermont-
Ferrand
○

Limoges
○

Lyon ○

ITALY

Bordeaux
○

Sarragachies
○

Toulouse ○

Montpellier
○

Nice ○

MONACO

Marseille ○

Perpignan ○

Ajaccio ○

SPAIN

100 km

A vine classified as a historic monument

A vineyard planted in Gers (France) around 1820

Uniquely, crops have now been listed on the French Inventory of Historic Monuments: this family garden at Sarragachies in Val d'Adour (Gers) was spared by phylloxera ... and from being uprooted.

'My grandmother's grandmother said they were already old vines,' recounts René Pédebernade who, at 87 years of age, was still attaching the vines to stakes with willow as his ancestors had always done. Each Sarragachies family used to have its own 'vine garden' planted with different red and white local varieties and produced its own wine – 'garage wine', as we'd say today.

This recently listed garden has several striking features. A quick glance reveals an ancient plantation in double rows, with the same stake supporting two plants, perhaps to save materials. The vines are arranged in 2 metre squares so that draft horses or oxen could pass by on all sides.

Experts from Sup Agro Montpellier, the Institut Français de la Vigne et du Vin (IFV) and the Institut National de la Recherche Agronomique (INRA) believe that the plantation dates from around 1820, and its sandy soil prevented the spread of phylloxera.

Finally, genetic analysis of these living relics reveals twenty different grape varieties, including seven that were completely unknown.

These vestiges survived uprooting because the family garden was not obliged to make a profit or follow new trends. Elsewhere the vines were replaced, either because the yield or the alcohol level was too low, or the growers complied with the authorised and certified clones. In the 1980s, the move to *appellation d'origine* was the motivation for uprooting and replanting many plots of land. Market forces, government incentives and agricultural advisers destroyed as much as phylloxera did.

Like a thousand other viticulturists, Jean-Pascal Pédebernade – René's son – sells his grapes to Plaimont Producteurs. 'We wanted to save these ancient vines for two reasons,' reveals Olivier Bourdet-Pees, the cooperative's general manager. 'We defend the local varieties because they have developed in local conditions, with the peculiarities of the terrain and climate. These varieties are adapted to our rainfall, which averages 1,000 millimetres a year. In 1950, the twenty most popular grape varieties accounted for 47 per cent of production, but today it's 86 per cent!' The genetic heritage and biodiversity are collapsing.

One of these unknown grape varieties found on Sarragachies land, known as Pédebernade No. 1, was tested in a micro-winemaking experiment. It yielded a wine of only 7° alcohol. For Bourdet-Pees, this is a hopeful sign: 'In Norway, the tax goes up with the level of alcohol. Low-alcohol wine is a future option.' So some people have understood that biodiversity favours adaptation to a changing and diverse market, new consumption patterns and global warming.

Male and female vines, in a wine-producing world where all currently registered varieties are hermaphrodite

At Sarragachies, there are even male vines – without grapes – and female vines. For a long time, growers have selected plants with the reproductive parts of both sexes: male (to fertilise) and female (to produce the clusters of grapes). So all currently registered varieties are hermaphrodite: neither male nor female.

© Pierrick Bourgault

UNITED-KINGDOM

NETHERLAND

BELGIUM

GERMANY

LUX.

Lille ○

○ Amiens

Cherbourg
○

Reims
○
**Champagne
Cattier**

○ Metz

Nancy ○

Strasbourg ○

Brest
○

Paris ■

Rennes
○

Orléans
○

Belfort ○

Dijon
○
**La Maison
Romane**

Besançon
○

SWITZERLAND

*La Table
Rouge*
○

Nantes
○

Poitiers ○

FRANCE

Limoges
○

Clermont-
Ferrand
○

Lyon ○

ITALY

L'Enclos
○

Bordeaux ○

Nice ○ MONACO

Toulouse ○

Montpellier ○

Marseille ○

Perpignan ○

Ajaccio ○

SPAIN

100 km

Vineyard horses

In recent years a few growers have again turned to traditional equine labour

Excavations of the vineyards at Pompeii have revealed that draught animals were widely used to work the vines, as borne out in Pliny the Elder's *Natural History*. Breeders did indeed train both oxen and horses, using the animals' massive strength to drag their carts and plough the fields.

The 20th century saw the last of the equine labour force. The First World War, started on horseback in 1914, ended four years later to the sound of backfiring combustion engines: tireless, powerful, and no need to feed them when not in use.

After the war, the factories that had built tanks assembled tractors to replace the missing farm labourers. If man and horse could plough between the rows at a rate of 0.1 hectare per hour, a tractor would be five times faster and therefore cheaper, even taking into account the cost of replacing the vines snapped by the tractor and the years of low yield from replacement plants. In total, man and horse can work 7–8 hectares of vines in a year, as against a tractor's 50 hectares.

The qualities of the animal are nevertheless obvious: beyond its environmental appeal (no machine to buy or fuel to import) and because it finds its energy locally (from pasture, cereals ...), farmers particularly appreciate its agricultural virtues:

Tillage. Although the weight under a carthorse's hoof can be greater per square centimetre than that of wide tyres at low pressure, a horse disturbs the soil less than a tractor, as demonstrated by Oronce de Beler (Burgundy, France): the tyre treads form a wall of compacted earth that obstructs earthworms and plant roots, so is detrimental to soil life and plant vitality. Engine vibration compacts the soil still more, even using a tracked vehicle. Working with a horse aerates the soil better, its consistency is noticeably finer and the vines can make the most of the *terroir*. De Beler also admires a horse's ability to work sloping ground, manoeuvre and turn around in a small space. Its intelligence and sense of balance make accidents less likely.

© Pierrick Bourgault

Gentle and precise. According to Philippe Chigard (Touraine, France), 'For special, old, rugged, difficult vines, the horse is superior to the tractor. Just like *haute couture*.' The powerful tractor regularly damages the trunks. The horse is gentler than the tractor and its work more sustainable, so that a grandfather can hand down to his grandson the vines he's planted, the ones that yield such high-quality juice.

A grower's contact with the vine using hand tools. De Beler designs his own tools: 'You're not sitting down, or in an air-conditioned cabin, but in direct contact with the soil. In a tractor, a man loses contact with his vines.' This is confirmed by Chigard: 'These tools resonate in your hands! The grower rediscovers why the vine is in trouble in one part of the plot and grows better elsewhere – pebbles, limestones, clays. What grandfather knew and we forgot.'

Organic farming. Working with a horse means organic farming. 'No question of spraying chemicals: horses have sensitive mucous membranes and they cough. We won't kit them out with gas masks like they did in 14/18!' laughs Chigard. 'Even nettle compost can be aggressive, the horse has to be washed down afterwards.' Chigard recommends spraying from a backpack wearing protective clothing.

Well-being. All agree on the pleasure to be had from the lack of engine noise and the sense of well-being offered by a horse in the vineyards, 'a little paradise'. The horse is a link in the trinity of man, animal and plant. Biodynamic winemaker Nicolas Joly claims that the elements within the vines enjoy the animal's presence.

How many estates use horses today? As they're sometimes used for festivities as well as regular work, it's difficult to name names. The best known is probably Château Latour, where horses are used on the 47 hectares of the mythical plot known as l'Enclos. Organic sprays are carried on the workers' backs, copper and sulphur arrive by tractor for rapid treatment if needed – so of course, the soil compaction argument is less convincing. On the edge of the forest of Amboise, Philippe Chigard keeps seven draught horses which work in the vineyards, and trains the cart drivers. Working horses in this way also helps to ensure the survival of endangered breeds such as the Auxois, Comtois, Ardennais and Breton …

In Burgundy, Oronce de Beler designs light hand tools intended for vineyard work.

In Champagne, the Cattier family (Chigny-les-Roses) also uses horses to carry out various tasks in the vineyards.

UNITED-KINGDOM

NETHERLAND

BELGIUM

GERMANY

Lille ○

LUX.

Amiens ○

Cherbourg
○

Reims ○

Metz ○

Paris ■

Nancy ○

Strasbourg ○

Brest
○

Rennes
○

Orléans
○

Belfort ○

Angers
○

Dijon ○

Besançon ○

Nantes
○

Coulée
de Serrant

SWITZERLAND

Poitiers
○

FRANCE

Limoges
○

Clermont-
Ferrand
○

Lyon ○

ITALY

Bordeaux ○

Nice
○

MONACO

Toulouse ○

Montpellier
○

Marseille ○

Perpignan ○

Ajaccio ○

SPAIN

N

100 km

Vineyard of the Coulée de Serrant

A course on biodynamic viticulture by Nicolas Joly

The aim of any controlled or protected designation of origin (appellation d'origine) is a consumer guarantee that the taste of a place will be expressed in its vine and wine. But according to Nicolas Joly, a winemaker near Angers (Loire region of western France), this laudable idea has come up against four obstacles: 'Herbicides kill the micro-organisms in the soil that allow the plants to feed. If I bound and gagged a guy and surrounded him with good food, he couldn't eat it. Secondly, fertilisers replace the growth linked to the soil with chemicals, which are salts. If you take in too much salt, you'll be thirsty and drink more water, which is why the growth encouraged by chemical fertilisers is mainly due to water. The third consequence of this imbalance is that the excess water causes various diseases, such as mildew or fungal infections. So pesticides that affect the whole organism were invented. The harvest is plentiful but lacks the imprint of the soil or the climate. The fourth pitfall is cellar technology, which makes up for any agricultural deficiencies without the consumer knowing. I'm thinking particularly of those terrible aromatic yeasts (there are over 300) that add a taste of citrus or blackcurrant: in short, wines that can be copied all over the world as they're deprived of their origins.'

To address these inbuilt obstacles, Nicolas Joly has come up with the idea of biodynamic agriculture, or 'dynamic biology'. This approach is not new: around 1920, German agronomists who were worried about modern technology and the effect of fertilisers on soil fertility asked the advice of 'anthroposophic' philosophers such as Austrian-born Rudolf Steiner, who in 1924 launched 'biodynamic' farming and gave a series of lectures on agriculture. Today, the word biodynamics applies mainly to wine: combining two positive terms, it designates agricultural practices that are 'in harmony with nature', thus reassuring the consumer.

Naturally, winemakers who practise biodynamics use organic farming methods: no chemical fertilisers or synthetic pesticides in the vineyard, and fermentation using fewer products than for 'conventional' wine. But biodynamic winemakers also make up extraordinary 'concoctions': plant infusions such as horsetail or 'nettle compost' as a spray, or 'horn manure' obtained by rotting dung in a cow's horn for a few months. These substances 'energised' in water are used diluted to an almost homeopathic degree.

Biodynamic winemakers also respect the lunar calendar, with its 'root' or 'leaf' days indicated for this or that operation. Other examples of curious practices: playing music in the vineyards and the bottling plants (see p. 101) for its supposed influence on the vines and the wine; refusing to cut the ends off the stems as other growers do when pruning, to stop foliage growth and concentrate on the grapes.

For Nicolas Joly, biodynamics is neither a list of recipes nor a fashionable marketing ploy, nor is it poetic licence. He is renowned in the wine world for having converted his vineyard of Coulée de Serrant, near Angers, to biodynamics in 1984. Since then he's travelled the world, teaching this radically different vision of agriculture.

With its 7 hectares, the Coulée de Serrant is not only one of the smallest wine appellations, but also the property of the family of Nicolas Joly, a pioneer of biodynamic viticulture.

How can a weak herbal infusion combat plant diseases?

Nicolas Joly: Conventional agriculture affects life by physical means, such as the addition of potash or nitrogen. Biodynamics works at another level: energy. Farmers know very well that their crop grows because of photosynthesis (taking water out of the equation), i.e. from the energy that the plant captures. Biodynamics favours this reception system: it doesn't act at the physical level but just before, when the plant takes in these forces and transforms them into matter.

So is the natural link disturbed?

N.J: Yes, because thousands of satellites and antennae saturate the atmosphere. Every mobile phone, every GPS, generates frequencies that are close to cosmic, so they disorientate the system of life on Earth. It's even worse than the 50 hertz high-voltage lines because a false note is so much more disturbing when it's close to the true note.

What danger do these frequencies represent?

N.J: Many current diseases. We're made up of vibrations: health is the balance of thousands of micro-rhythms. Imposing a dominant one disrupts them all. Young people who are born in this environment are at risk of developing health problems. This has to stop, even though there's a market for these information technologies. Depending on your genetic makeup and your diet, you'll be more or less resistant.

How should agriculture evolve?

N.J: Agriculture will once again become the art of linking a place to the forces needed by plants and animals to best express their potential and that of their terroir. Add nothing, just let things happen. You'll get the true taste of a place, of a soil, that the vine captures through its roots and leaves like an antenna. Each variety will do so differently, just as three artists facing the same landscape will paint three different pictures.

How important are low yields?

N.J: Performance is the key. Returning to what the ground is capable of yielding, there would be less disease and better quality products, at no extra cost in chemicals. Of course, it depends on your initial investment and therefore the purchase price of the vines.

What do you think of organic?

N.J: Organic is the first step, avoiding the input of disruptive synthetic substances. We don't live on matter but on the energy it contains. When you eat chaotic and disrupted material, you too are disrupted. Organic says to nature: we respect you and you do your work. Organic is great, but unfortunately it's not enough today.

Doesn't biodynamics have a placebo effect on consumers?

N.J: That effect is mainly on the farmer and the plants! The same treatment carried out by a bio enthusiast and someone who couldn't care less will have different effects. Like a gardener's green fingers – as yet unexplained – this placebo effect is hugely empowering to man, whose mental and emotional capacities set us above the mineral, plant and animal kingdoms. Man is the conductor. The musicians are the place, the climate, the landscape and the geology.

What are its limits?

N.J: Biodynamic certification does not guarantee that this is reflected in the wine. In biodynamics, the results vary according to the grower's understanding and depth of commitment, like the music played by a musician or on a particular instrument. Even certification by a serious organisation like Demeter doesn't guarantee the full expression of biodynamic preparations.

How do you judge the quality of a wine?

N.J: Open a bottle, try it, put it on one side, then try it again the next day. With a conventional wine, the life fades from it. Biodynamic wine is like a young person who needs to be awakened: it explodes with life. The rush of oxygen awakens the living, but if the wine hasn't enough life in it, it dies. This also tests whether it'll keep for ten years in the cellar.

© Pierrick Bourgault

UNITED-KINGDOM

NETHERLAND

Lille ○

BELGIUM

GERMANY

○ Amiens

LUX.

Cherbourg
○

○ Reims

○ Metz

Paris
■

Nancy ○

Strasbourg ○

Brest
○

Rennes
○

Orléans
○

Belfort ○

Dijon ○

Besançon
○

SWITZERLAND

Nantes
○

Poitiers ○

FRANCE

Limoges
○

Clermont-
Ferrand
○

Lyon ○

ITALY

Château
Blissa
○

Bordeaux ○

Nice
○

MONACO

Toulouse ○

Montpellier
○

Marseille ○

Perpignan ○

Ajaccio ○

SPAIN

100 km

Bordeaux made with dry ice

An innovative technique that is spectacularly chemical-free

No chemicals and entirely natural: the thick cloud that emanates from the barrel is only liquid carbon dioxide, the CO_2 in the air we breathe. On the Côtes de Bourg, near Bordeaux (France), Stéphane Destrade uses dry ice to macerate part of his *Château de Blissa* harvest in order to keep the fruit fresh. *How it's done*: Destrade first leaves his grapes for a classic cold soak (cryomaceration) in new oak barrels at a temperature of 6 °C for six days. Every six hours, dry ice is added so that the temperature remains low. The grapes soak in the cold for a few days before fermentation, hence the name of the method. Cryomaceration, which is often used for white wines, gives more fruity aromas than if the fermentation had begun at room temperature straight after harvesting – just as a casserole stewed slowly at low temperature will taste better than one using a pressure cooker.

Of course, this method is expensive in storage space and electricity for cooling (here with dry ice): respect for fruity, delicate aromas comes at a price.

Six days after the harvest, Destrade pours another measure of dry ice (liquid carbon dioxide at −78.5 °C) over the grapes. An impressive white cloud rises from the barrel and the berries burst. 'This process gives mellower tannins and sexier wines,' comments Stéphane Toutoundji, oenologist at Blissa. 'The balance is more interesting, the wines more colourful and fruity. The ice is like a sorbet, extracting the best from the fruit.'

Another advantage is that carbon dioxide saturation displaces oxygen around the grapes, preventing damage from oxidation.

During the six days of fermentation at 18 °C, the mixture of berries, juice and skin is stirred with a stick (an operation called *pigeage*) and the must is pumped up (*remontage*) so that fermentation and colour is homogeneous. As in making tea, the more the mixture is stirred, the stronger it gets; and the more material extracted, the more tannic and colourful the juice.

The wine is then set aside while the Quintessence cooper refits the lids of the barrels in which the wine will age. Destrade was a London banker who left everything to take over the family property and create a wine that pleases him: 'fruity, very fresh and pure, with silky tannins'.

A new-generation wine, rare in traditional Bordeaux wineries.

© Tonnellerie Quintessence

UNITED-KINGDOM

NETHERLAND

BELGIUM

GERMANY

Lille o

LUX.

Amiens o

Cherbourg
o

Reims o

Metz o

Paris
■

Nancy
o

Strasbourg o

Brest
o

Champagne

Rennes
o

Belfort o

Orléans
o

Dijon o

Besançon
o

SWITZERLAND

Nantes
o

Poitiers o

FRANCE

Limoges
o

Clermont-
Ferrand
o

Lyon o

ITALY

Bordeaux o

Nice o

MONACO

Toulouse o

Montpellier o

Marseille o

Perpignan o

Ajaccio o

SPAIN

N

100 km

Pink champagne: a very rare exception to rosé regulations

Why does champagne come from a black grape?
What is Blanc de Noirs? And red champagne?

First remarkable fact: 90 per cent of champagne bottles contain white wine, while 70 per cent of the vineyards of the Champagne region of France are planted with black grapes. Pinot Noir in particular is used for the great Burgundy reds, but also Blanc de Noirs (literally 'white of blacks') by carefully avoiding colouring the pressed juice with the skins.

Wouldn't it make more sense to make a white wine from white grapes? No doubt, but Pinot Noir gives a structured framework and a delicate bouquet that is full and intense, with fine aromatic complexity: all characteristic of the great champagnes. The harvest is carried out by hand, whole bunches carefully transported in crates and quickly pressed: harvesting machines are banned as they suck in the grapes and crush them, and the skin would stain the juice. 'A very light champagne shows the skill of the winemaker. For a long while, pink champagne was considered flawed, a sacrilege,' asserts Hubert de Billy of Champagne Pol Roger. Blanc de Blancs designates champagnes made only from the white Chardonnay grape that covers the remaining 30 per cent of the region's vineyards.

Second remarkable fact: to make their rosé (10 per cent of production), the Champagne winemakers add a little local red to the white. This mix guarantees precise colour control, an important feature for a fashionable luxury product. But isn't mixing white and red wines to make pink wine banned in theory? True, but as a second fermentation takes place in the bottles to make foam (when still wine becomes sparkling), the organoleptic characteristics of champagne aren't the same as a straightforward mix of wines of two colours.

Automated remuage (riddling) of champagne bottles, using a machine known as a gyropalette, takes a few days (Bouvay-Ladubay, Saumur, France)

By hand, with the bottles on pupitres, a similar operation takes several weeks (Champagne Cattier, Montagne de Reims, France)

Exception to the above facts: a few pink champagnes (1 per cent of production) come from saigneés, i.e. from 'bleeding' the Pinot Noir skin colour into the juice). The grapes are left to macerate overnight and pressed the next day.

Thanks to public approbation, winemakers have finally seen pink champagne as a noble wine and there's even a Pol Roger rosé.

Finally, to top it all, as the law doesn't ban nuanced shades of pink, some winemakers push their luck even further, going as far as red // sparkling //champagne (a few still reds are produced in the Champagne region). In the 19th century, this curiosity was achieved by adding 25–35 per cent of red wine, followed by a red *liqueur d'expédition*. Some winemakers prepare bottles of this 'very dark rosé' for home consumption, as red champagne doesn't officially exist (the trade organisation – Comité Interprofessionnel du Vin de Champagne – would expel any winemaker who dared to publicise it).

Château Bouvet-Ladubay in Touraine (Loire valley) makes a *demi-sec* (medium-dry) sparkling red called *Rubis*. Sparkling red is more widespread in Italy, especially Lambrusco and the wines of Oltrepò Pavese ('Pavia across the Po' in Lombardy), such as Bonarda.

Champagne, an English invention?

In the Middle Ages, monks all over France cultivated vines and made wine from the grapes to celebrate the Eucharist, but also for sale. The climate of Champagne is colder than that of the Burgundian abbeys, but the same grape varieties – Pinot Noir and Chardonnay – were chosen. To facilitate trade and move the barrels, the vines were astutely planted near waterways (Marne, Aube, Aisne) with their confluence at Paris and Rouen. From 816 to 1825, the coronation of thirty-three kings of France at Reims meant unparalleled prestige for the local wine, even though the grapes didn't always ripen and the wine from some vineyards turned out rather acidic.

From their neighbours in Champagne, the English bought barrels of this wine: it was normally still, without bubbles, and with added sugar cane to soften the acidity. Pierre Pérignon, known as Dom Pérignon, a Benedictine monk (1639–1715), observed a mysterious phenomenon that only the work of Louis Pasteur (1822–1895), who revealed the action of yeasts, was able to explain: with the cold of winter the activity of the micro-organisms in the barrels stops, only to restart when the temperature rises. The addition of sugar feeds the yeasts and activates them. If the wine is already bottled, the bottles will explode: they are unable to withstand the pressure exerted by the carbon dioxide from this new fermentation.

The pragmatic English could produce stronger glass thanks to the high temperatures achieved from burning coal, while the French were still heating their foundries with wood. For these reasons (added sugar and resistant bottles), several writers maintain that champagne is an English rather than a French invention.

The method of making champagne remains unchanged: the first fermentation in an open tank gives a still wine, the second is carried out in solid bottles with the addition of sugar beet* (*liqueur de tirage*).** The bottles are closed with a crown cap, like a beer bottle, and the second fermentation begins. The carbon dioxide can't escape and forms bubbles in the wine.

To remove the unsightly dead yeast or lees, the bottles are stacked on a rack and gradually inclined so that the sediment falls towards the neck. The process known as disgorgement involves opening each bottle to eliminate this deposit and then nimbly topping up the level with *liqueur d'expédition*.***

Whether from beet or cane, the sugar added to launch the second fermentation is sucrose. For one of his blends, winemaker Fabrice Pouillon use sugar from very ripe grape juice of the same plot and the same vintage. So his champagne is entirely local, with no external ingredients.

The blend is known as *Chemin de bois*.

Sugar beet was developed in 1811 by Benjamin Delessert, to overcome the blockade of West Indian sugar imposed by the English at war with Napoleon.

**A syrupy mixture of wine, sugar and yeast added to cause a secondary fermentation that induces carbonation.*

***A mixture of wine and sugar added to balance the acidity or to give the wine a degree of sweetness, if required.*

Belgian and English copies of Champagne

In Belgium, Ruffus makes its sparkling wine using the same grape varieties (Chardonnay, Pinot Noir, Pinot Meunier) and the same traditional method as in Champagne. And to the south of London (Kent, Sussex, Hampshire), the same chalky soil and warming climate mean that England, an avid consumer of sparkling wines, can produce cuvées comparable to Champagne.

© Pierrick Bourgault

© Pierrick Bourgault

UNITED-KINGDOM

NETHERLAND

Lille o

BELGIUM

GERMANY

Amiens o

LUX.

Cherbourg
o

Reims o

Metz o

Nancy o

Strasbourg o

Brest
o

Paris ■

Rennes
o

Orléans
o

Belfort o

Dijon o

Besançon o

SWITZERLAND

Nantes
o

Jura

Poitiers o

FRANCE

Clermont-
Ferrand
o

Limoges
o

Lyon o

ITALY

Bordeaux o

Nice o

MONACO

Toulouse o

Montpellier o

Marseille o

Perpignan o

Ajaccio o

SPAIN

N

100 km

Yellow wine

Unique winemaking methods and distinctive flavours

Oenologists are strict about this: wine must be protected from oxidation as it causes a rancid taste and a stale smell, or even turns the wine to vinegar. Oxygen is life: bacteria, moulds and yeasts can't survive without it. Everybody knows that a bottle that has been opened and forgotten for a few weeks may no longer be drinkable. Oxygen is the bane of all winemakers, the reason why barrels are filled to the brim. As the wine evaporates because of the tiny amounts of oxygenation through the pores of the wood, the barrels are topped up regularly. This evaporation is poetically known as 'the angels' share', and the topping up as ullage. Very few wines take the risk of ignoring the top-up rule. In the Jura, the local Savagnin grape yields a prized white wine. A few winemakers age it in a partially full barrel: an intriguing veil of the *Saccharomyces cerevisiae* yeast then develops on the surface.

After six years and three months, on the first weekend in February, the barrel is opened to great celebration. The wine is bottled in 0.62 litre *clavelins*. Unlike the conventional 0.75 litre bottle, this unusual measure is a tribute to 'the angels' share', i.e. the liquid evaporated over the years from a litre of wine, but it seems that the clavelin also owes something to an English-style bottle.

During its seventy-five months under a veil of yeast, the white wine takes on a bronze colour which is described as *jaune* (yellow). It looks like a sweet wine but turns out to be perfectly dry, with no residual sugars. The taste is reminiscent of walnuts, with a wonderful finish from the pronounced aromatics that have developed.

Another unusual feature is that it keeps for decades, even for hundreds of years, and an open bottle can remain for some considerable time on the shelf without unpleasant oxidation: the wine is already past that stage. The International Organisation of Vine and Wine classes it as a 'speciality wine'.

Note that some wineries, such as Overnoy and Puffeney, leave their *vin jaune* ageing in the barrel even longer than the six years and three months authorised by the appellation.

Other wines that "take the veil"

Spanish sherry (*xeres*) is another example of wine aged using the *sous voile* [lit. under the veil] technique. Some winemakers in the south of France are also trying it, such as Robert and Bernard Plageoles (Gaillac) and the Jorel estate (Maury) with its *La Garrigue* wine from the rare Macabeu grape, which is aged for ten years.

Don't confuse *vin jaune* with the other Jura speciality, Macvin, made by adding marc (grape brandy distilled from the fermented mash, also known as marc) to fortify grape juice. Macvin comes in three colours: red, rosé and white.

UNITED-KINGDOM

NETHERLAND

Lille o

BELGIUM

GERMANY

Amiens o

LUX.

Cherbourg o

o Reims

o Metz

Paris ■

Nancy o

Strasbourg o

Brest o

Rennes o

Orléans o

Belfort o

Dijon o

Besançon o

SWITZERLAND

Nantes o

Poitiers o

FRANCE

Limoges o

Clermont-
Ferrand o

Lyon o

ITALY

Bordeaux o

○ *Padirac*

Toulouse o

Montpellier o

Nice o

MONACO

Marseille o

Perpignan o

Ajaccio o

SPAIN

100 km

The wine of the Padirac Cave

A wine matured at the bottom of a 75-metre-deep hole

In the Dordogne region lies the magnificent Gouffre de Padirac cave measuring 75 metres deep and 33 metres wide. This ancient cave, the chasm and its underground river were discovered in 1889 by Edouard-Alfred Martel. The cave's ceiling naturally collapsed at an undetermined time.

To celebrate the 130th anniversary of its discovery, the management behind the Gouffre de Padirac teamed up with the Clos Triguedina wine estate in 2019 to launch its first 130th Anniversary Cuvée, made from century-old Malbec vines from the Cahors appellation.

Some 500 numbered bottles of Cuvée Probus are placed in the chasm, 103 metres below ground, to mature for a year. The conditions are ideal: 97 per cent humidity and a perfectly stable temperature of 13°C. There's no risk of the cork drying out. The unique environment seems to offer an ideal setting. Isn't there a saying that good produce is born in beautiful landscapes? The results were as good as expected, and the experiment was repeated with a second and third series of the 130th Anniversary Cuvée. The experiment will be repeated every year.

© C.Gerigk-SESdePadirac

CUVÉE DES 130 ANS

À l'occasion du 130ème anniversaire de sa découverte,
le Gouffre de Padirac s'est associé au Clos Triguedina pour
créer une cuvée spéciale : la Cuvée Probus des 130 ans.

Près de 500 bouteilles et 24 magnums de cette cuvée de
vignes centenaires pur Malbec en AOC ont été enfouis ici
en mai 2020.

À 103 mètres sous terre, les conditions de conservation
sont exceptionnelles : un taux d'humidité de 98% et une
température de 13° toute l'année.

Le vin se bonifiera dans cette cave naturelle au centre de la
Terre durant un an, jusqu'au printemps 2021.

Created in 1976 by the Baldès family of Clos Triguedina, a family of winegrowers since 1830, the Cuvée Probus was named in honour of Emperor Probus (c. 232–282 CE), who is said to have authorised the cultivation of vines in Gaul. Two centuries earlier, an edict by Domitian banned the cultivation of vines in the region, to protect the winegrowers of the Italian peninsula.

Now it is possible to taste the 130th Anniversary Cuvée at the bottom of the Gouffre de Padirac as part of a VIP tour, and it is also on sale in the delicatessen of the Gouffre de Padirac, called the "Kiosque du Gouffre", and at Clos Triguedina. Visitors can even compare it with a Probus matured in a cellar.

UNITED-KINGDOM

NETHERLAND

BELGIUM

GERMANY

Lille

Amiens

LUX.

Cherbourg

Reims

Metz

Paris

Nancy

Strasbourg

Brest

Rennes

Orléans

Belfort

Dijon

Besançon

Nantes

SWITZERLAND

Clos Cristal

Poitiers

FRANCE

Clermont-
Ferrand

Limoges

Lyon

ITALY

Bordeaux

Nice

MONACO

Toulouse

Montpellier

Marseille

Perpignan

Ajaccio

SPAIN

N

100 km

Le Clos Cristal

Vines that grow through walls

You could say this is a full-bodied story. Born in 1837 in Turquant near Saumur, Antoine Cristal made his fortune in the textile industry before returning to settle in his native region, which is renowned for its white wines (red grapes tended to ripen poorly there, although that was before global warming ...). Antoine Cristal was a republican and freethinker, and a friend of Georges Clemenceau, who visited him regularly.

As a novice winegrower, Cristal quickly realised vines and roots needed moisture to thrive, while the grapes needed sun and warmth to ripen. In other words, the vines needed to have their roots in the shade and their heads in the sun. In 1890, he acquired around 10 hectares in the commune of Champigny and surrounded the land with walls – hence the name Clos Cristal ('clos' meaning enclosed in French). The walls created a special microclimate which was warmer and sheltered from the wind. Cristal had several kilometres of walls built, with holes in them. The vines were planted to the north, where the humidity was persistent. They grew against the walls and, halfway up, continued through the holes. The shoots, foliage and grape bunches grew facing south. As a result, the vines benefit from the sun's reflection during the day, as rays of light bounce off the walls and stimulate the backs of the leaves, promoting photosynthesis, the plant's metabolism, and the supply of mineral compounds to the grapes. The heat stored during the day is redistributed at night, protecting the fragile young leaves from spring frosts, and the walls also enable the vines to continue to ripen for almost an extra month at the end of the season. The Clos Cristal thus became an experimental site for Cabernet Franc to flourish.

Cristal dreamt that his Clos de Saumur-Champigny could compete with great red wines. He donated the Clos in 1928 to the Hospices de Saumur, a listed estate which had recently been taken over by the Robert et Marcel winery (part of the Alliance Loire group of cooperatives). The new management team recounts that Cristal's wines travelled the world, from the great courts of Europe to Japan and Russia, not to mention the finest restaurants in France. King Edward VII of England is said to have loved them, as did Claude Monet.

In 2017, a little less than 5 hectares were in production. The vineyard was not in very good condition and some vines had to be replanted. The aim is now to tend the vines so that they can produce 30 hectolitres per hectare, which corresponds to a modest yield for the Saumur-Champigny designation. This is why current production does not exceed 5,000 bottles, which are all individually numbered.

Philippe Faure-Brac, who won the title of World's Best Sommelier in 1992, described the Clos Cristal wine as follows: 'Very beautiful colour, fine, delicate nose, with notes of red cherry and sloe. A lovely woody touch with aromas of vanilla, cinnamon, and sweet spices. Fine, integrated tannins.'

The buildings in the Clos Cristal are reminiscent of the walls built in Montreuil (Île-de-France) to help peach trees ripen.
The Montreuil 'peach walls' made the town on the outskirts of Paris famous.

UNITED-KINGDOM

NETHERLAND

BELGIUM

GERMANY

Charbonnay ○ Lille

LUX.

○ Amiens

Cherbourg
○

○ Reims

○ Metz

Paris
■

Nancy ○

Strasbourg ○

Brest
○

Rennes
○

Orléans
○

Belfort ○

Dijon ○

Besançon
○

SWITZERLAND

Nantes
○

Poitiers ○

FRANCE

Clermont-
Ferrand
○

Lyon ○

ITALY

Limoges
○

Bordeaux ○

Nice ○ MONACO

Toulouse ○

Montpellier ○

Marseille ○

Ajaccio ○

Perpignan ○

SPAIN

N

100 km

Charbonnay

Vines that grow on a slag heap in northern France

Northern France is home to many slag heaps: slag from mining operations used to be piled up to form artificial hills, usually conical, until 1990. When the French mining company Charbonnages de France closed down, these steeply sloping heaps were handed over to local municipalities and departments. In 2016, a 'chain' of 78 slag heaps was even listed as a national heritage site.

Today, these heaps are almost entirely abandoned, left at the mercy of wild grasses, or grazing goats that help preserve their emblematic blackness. They are like islands of infertility that tractors cannot reach because of their steep slopes.

However, in 2009, Olivier Pucek, a local born at the foot of the imposing slag heap at Haillicourt (in the Pas-de-Calais department) and a descendant of miners, suggested planting a slag-heap vineyard to the town hall covering the area where his childhood pile is located. The idea seemed bizarre, even far-fetched, especially as growing vines was not authorised by the authorities in this 'non-wine-producing department', except 'on an experimental basis'.

Pucek, who already had 3 hectares of vines in the Charente region, teamed up with Henri Jammet, a Charente winemaker renowned for his chardonnay. Their wine would be called charbonnay, an obvious reference to the coal that made the region so rich in the past ('charbon' means coal in French). 'The mayor and his team welcomed us and agreed to invest alongside us. The department has even become the owner of this land, which slopes at 60–70, sometimes even 80 degrees.'

The two winegrowers saw the obstacles as an advantage. The poor, draining soil is perfect for vines, the dark colour keeps the heat in, and the altitude provides valuable ventilation to limit mould. In 2011, they courageously planted 2,000 vines on the southern slope, then another 1,000 to make a total of 3,000 today. These steep, south-facing slopes also provide maximum sunshine for each vine.

In 2016, Europe finally compelled the French government to allow all its regions to grow vines.

Today, half of this one-hectare plot has been planted. The grapes are vinified on site to produce more than 1,000 bottles of Charbonnay a year, and it has been a great success.

Although it remains the first wine produced in the Pas-de-Calais region and it is the only one made from vines planted on a slag heap, it has given others ideas. Some neighbouring farmers of limestone slopes not favourable for wheat have turned them into vineyards, and a group of winegrowers in the Hauts-de-France region have launched their own brand, called 'Les 130'.

© Sylvain Beucler

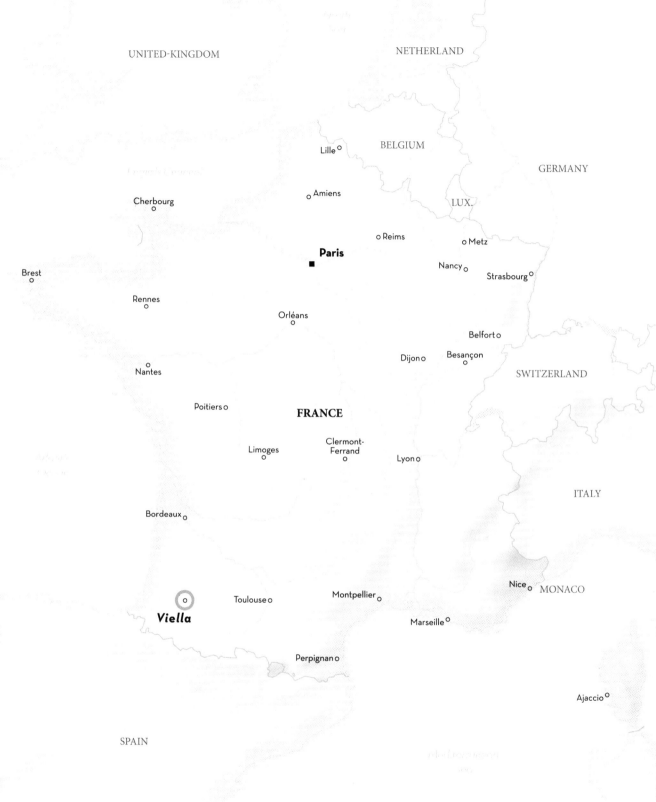

UNITED-KINGDOM

NETHERLAND

BELGIUM

GERMANY

Lille

LUX.

Amiens

Cherbourg

Reims

Metz

Paris

Nancy

Strasbourg

Brest

Rennes

Orléans

Belfort

Nantes

Dijon

Besançon

SWITZERLAND

Poitiers

FRANCE

Clermont-
Ferrand

Lyon

Limoges

ITALY

Bordeaux

Viella

Toulouse

Montpellier

Nice

MONACO

Marseille

Perpignan

Ajaccio

SPAIN

N

100 km

New Year's Eve harvests

Every 31 December, the growers of Plaimont Producteurs
end the year with a festival and nocturnal harvests open to all

Viella (Gers, France). Over 500 visitors, young and old, are warming themselves over burning branches. At 7.30 in the evening they grab their secateurs and baskets for the final harvest of the year: a half-hour by candlelight before rejoining their respective celebrations. Members of the Plaimont Producteurs cooperative are proud to show off their craft and launch the New Year festivities.

The Pacherenc de la Saint-Sylvestre vintage was launched in 1991 when the viticulturists, caught out by an exceptional frost, decided to leave the grapes on the vine until 31 December.

Dried by the wind, exposed to the autumn sun and cold nights, the sugars concentrate in the grapes, preventing them from freezing. The skin thickens as they mature, so they keep longer on the vine. In other appellation zones, this passerillage* is carried out in a barn or shed with the clusters hung on wires.

The vines of the *Pacherenc du Vic-Bihl* zone cover 250 hectares between Gers, the Pyrénées-Atlantiques and the Hautes-Pyrénées. The grape varieties are local – Petit and Gros Manseng. From October to December, in four or five passes (*tries*), the growers harvest the ripe grapes for different wines and the grape juice is fermented to medium-sweet (*moelleux*) depending on the batch. The October grape yields aromas of fresh fruits, citrus, grapefruit; the November grape (around St Albert's Day) evokes candied fruits, spices; the December grape is reminiscent of dried fruits – almonds, walnuts, honey ... Thanks to the acidity of these varieties and the cool climate, the wine remains balanced and not too sweet. A medium-sweet redolent with flavour and history.

This harvest festival was originally held even later, after midnight on 31 December. The Plaimont cooperative used to erect a marquee to accommodate the revellers, but this was expensive in both rent and insurance and a heavy workload for the volunteers. Nowadays the harvest begins in the early evening, so children can take part. It's no longer the first harvest of the year, but the last. The celebrations begin in the morning with a snack among the vines that will be harvested that evening. Demonstrations by draught horses evoke the work of bygone days, while winemakers tell of their craft and show visitors around the rows of vines, covered with netting to protect them from hungry birds. You can taste the overripe grapes to enjoy their sugar content. The village resonates to the sound of wandering musicians and local versions of *boules* such as *jeu de quilles* and *palet gascon*, while horse-drawn carriages offer rides. Vine grafters, wood turners, wool spinners, grinders and *espélouquères* (who strip the cobs from the corn) all demonstrate their age-old skills to the new generations. Not to mention tasting the different *tries of Pacherenc* and other wines.

© Pierrick Bourgault

UNITED-KINGDOM

NETHERLAND

BELGIUM

GERMANY

Lille

Amiens

LUX.

Cherbourg

Reims

Metz

Paris

Nancy

Strasbourg

Brest

Grémillet

Rennes

Belfort

Orléans

Dijon

Besançon

SWITZERLAND

Nantes

Poitiers

FRANCE

Limoges

Clermont-
Ferrand

Lyon

ITALY

Bordeaux

Nice

MONACO

Toulouse

Montpellier

Marseille

Perpignan

Ajaccio

SPAIN

100 km

Night harvest
at Champagne Grémillet

An evening in the vineyards, 'because work is also fun!'

'It all started one night in September,' says Anne Grémillet, the founder's daughter. 'We had a nightclub, with a big spotlight that we pointed at the vines. The light was so good that we thought we could harvest even at night.' Anne and her brother, Jean-Christophe, the cellar master, created a special cuvée in black glass, certified by a bailiff. Every year at harvest time they organise a festive Saturday evening to remind everyone that work is also fun.

Friends and customers join the employed harvesters and the seasonal workers, who come mainly from Poland. The festive harvest encourages transparency and fosters the good public relations so essential to farming.

On the Saturday evening during the 10 days or so that the harvest lasts, the Grémillet family invite the public in the late afternoon to visit the wine cellars, the tasting room, the wine library, and the museum of old tools. Three vintages of champagne are served as an aperitif, followed by dinner with the grape harvesters: a hearty meal with vegetable soup, pâté and raw vegetables, beef bourguignon, cheese and ice cream. Burgundy is just around the corner: we're in the Côte des Bar, to the south of the Champagne designation. The large family dining room feeds around a hundred people from 6 a.m. to 11 p.m.

At the end of the meal, everyone happily heads for the gates of Clos Rocher. Strong spotlights and individual headlamps help the one-night harvesters and experienced seasonal workers fill buckets with bunches of Pinot Noir, in an international atmosphere. The festive harvest provides an opportunity for dialogue, as it does at Plaimont on 31 December (see p. 65). During the meal, no subject is taboo; conversations include how hard it is to find staff, pesticides, climate change, and more. The man in charge of the vines talks about the burnt grapes destroyed by the heat wave and observes that the harvest begins earlier and earlier: 'I've been working in the vineyards for 35 years, and I've already seen several harvests in August. Something is happening. As a benefit, we no longer suffer from powdery mildew, and we don't need to treat the vines.'

As a result of this experiment, the estate has received a HVE (High Environmental Value) certification. Created in 1978, it now produces 500,000 bottles a year from 50 hectares.

With their oenological expertise, and after several years of night-time wine tastings, the family honestly concluded that there are no significant differences with daytime harvesting, but the experiment has been going on for the last 15 years or so, 'because the festivities bring the teams together.'

The oldest vine in the world

A 400-year-old vine that escaped every war

In Rhineland-Palatinate, a region where vines have been cultivated since Roman times, some 20 km from the border with France is the village of Rhodt unter Rietburg, famous for its villa Ludwigshöhe built for Ludwig I of Bavaria.

It is also known for a far more modest site: a historic vineyard barely visible from the road and believed to be the oldest in the world still harvested today.

A commemorative plaque certifies its age: over 400 years. Pascal Oberhofer, the young winemaker in charge of the land, refers to 'old church books' that indicate the age of these low, thick, gnarled vines. According to local tradition, these 270 Gewurztraminer and Sylvaner vines were planted before the Thirty Years War (1618–1648). Oberhofer manages the 25 hectares of his family estate, carefully preserving this ancestral vineyard, which continues to produce a white grape, vinified dry and sold in 37.5-centilitre bottles encased in a spectacular wood and cardboard display case.

This historic vineyard is one of the highlights of the Southern Wine Route.

A dozen or so red grapes also grow here and there, but are not vinified.

It is a rose garden ('rosengarten' in German) on the estate that gives this historic vineyard its name: Rhodter Rosengarten.

© Pierrick Bourgault

© Pierrick Bourgault

DENMARK

Kiel

Rostock

Lübeck

Bremerhaven   Hamburg   Schwerin

Bremen

NETHERLANDS

POLAND

■ **Berlin**

Osnabrück   Hannover   Potsdam

Magdeburg

Dortmund   Göttingen   Halle

GERMANY   Leipzig

Düsseldorf   Kassel   Görlitz

Köln   Erfurt   Dresden

Aachen

Bonn

BELG.

Koblenz

Frankfurt-
am-Main

Mainz   Bamberg   CZECH
REP.

LUX.   Trier   Würzburg

Mannheim   Nürnberg

Sarrebruck

Regensburg

**Domaine
Friedrich Becker**
Stuttgart   Passau

FRANCE   Ulm   Augsburg

Munich

Freiburg-
Briesgau

Ravensburg

N

SWITZERLAND

LIECH.   AUSTRIA

100 km

Friedrich Becker estate

A 'censored' German wine made from French vines

When Friedrich Becker, a winegrower from Schweigen-Rechtenbach (Germany), takes visitors on a tour of his estate, he never fails to stop in the middle of the vines. What's so remarkable about these vines and their almost identical rows, gently swaying in the wind? Nothing at all. Today, everything is peaceful. The border that was the scene of so much bloody fighting, ambushes, and machine-gun fire, passes through these vines, perfectly unnoticed.

The land has long been coveted. Becker explains: 'The Romans had already recognised the Palatinate's exceptional sunshine and brought olive and almond trees here. The forest protects us from the frost. To keep buildings healthy, the ancients planted vines to pump water from the foundations.'

The land has an ambiguous border. The armistice of 1918 and the Franco-German treaties concerning the demarcation had to tackle one tricky detail: the precious forest was donated in the 8th century by Pepin the Short to the abbey of Wissembourg. The forest had obtained from Otto II a tax exemption, or *immunitas*, which gave rise to the forest's name: Mundat.

Fragmented after the defeat of Napoleon I, the forest was an ongoing bone of contention between France and Germany. In 1983, Chancellor Kohl and President Mitterrand finally signed an agreement: Mundat forest would remain German, but under French ownership. All that remained to be done was to find the 900 boundary markers erected along 100 km after the First World War. This required a good 10 years of research before the border was finally agreed in 1998.

Facing south and located in France, the Wissembourg hill has always been of interest to winegrowers. Many Germans rent or buy these vineyards, to vinify the grapes in their cellars 2 km away, on the German side.

About 60 per cent of the 30 hectares of Becker's estate is in France. While vines don't care about borders, the same can't be said for designations with strict territorial limits. Becker said: 'Our concern isn't with France, but with the German administration, and what we can put on our labels. We don't have the right to indicate the place where we grow our wine.'

That's why he prints the word 'Zensiert' (censored) on the labels of his bottles, which are both rare and renowned in Germany.

DENMARK

Kiel

Rostock

Lübeck

Bremerhaven   Hamburg   Schwerin

Bremen

NETHERLANDS

POLAND

Osnabrück   Hannover   Potsdam   ■ Berlin

Magdeburg

Dortmund   Göttingen   Halle

Düsseldorf   Kassel   GERMANY   Leipzig

Görlitz

Köln   Erfurt   Dresden

Aachen

Bonn

BELG.

Koblenz

Bremm   CZECH REP.

Frankfurt-am-Main

Mainz   Bamberg

Trier

LUX.   Würzburg   Nürnberg

Mannheim

Sarrebruck   Regensburg

Stuttgart   Passau

FRANCE   Ulm   Augsburg

Munich

Freiburg-Briesgau

Ravensburg

AUSTRIA

N

SWITZERLAND

LIECH.

100 km

Warrior vines

Vineyards perched on slopes of 65 degrees along the banks of the Moselle River, accessible on foot or by miniature monorail train only

With a gradient of up to 65 degrees, the vineyards on the slopes on the banks of the Moselle are among the steepest in the world.

In Bremm, Angelina Franzen and her husband Kilian cultivate around 10 hectares exclusively by hand. Every move is calculated: 'If the picker leans on the vines when walking through the vineyard, he runs the risk of causing ripe grapes to fall off. That's why we always start at the end: the picker picks the vine closest and moves on.'

Working in these sloped vineyards takes ten times longer than on the plains: 'Each hectare requires 1,200 to 2,000 hours of work per year, compared with 200 on the plains, and the walls have to be consolidated every three or four years, because the mountain moves. We have four year-round employees and five back-up workers from Poland and Romania for the grape harvest.'

A considerable workforce for just 10 hectares. Angelina smiles: 'Look at the state of the shoes!' They might be picking the grapes by hand, but it's the workers' feet that are put to the test on this terrain.

Another consequence of the operating costs is that many plots have been abandoned. Over the last century, the number of vineyards has halved. 'At €50,000 per hectare, these vineyards are the cheapest in Germany. But they're worth ten times as much on the plains.'

Today, there are just ten or so winegrowers left in the area. Of course, they have a tractor to get close to the plots of land, but all motorised equipment stops by the road: there are no machines for cultivating or harvesting. Spraying is done using a shared helicopter, between the yellow triangles that indicate the property limits. Red triangles indicate areas to be avoided.

The wealthiest winegrowers install a railway in their vineyards. The Franzens have two of these miniature 'locomotives' to access the vines and bring back the harvested crates.

© MaxAdams

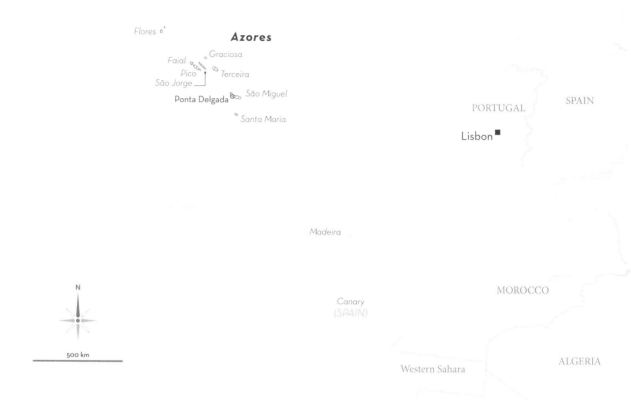

Azores

Flores

Graciosa

Faial
Pico
São Jorge
Terceira

São Miguel

Ponta Delgada

Santa Maria

PORTUGAL

SPAIN

Lisbon

Madeira

MOROCCO

N

Canary
(SPAIN)

500 km

Western Sahara

ALGERIA

The walled vines of the Azores

Volcanic soil for vines
inscribed on UNESCO's World Heritage List

Although this Portuguese archipelago in the Atlantic, 1,500 kilometres from Europe, is now more famous for its high atmospheric pressure (Azores High) than for its wine, the islanders have managed to get the best out of the small amount of cultivable land in the volcanic mountainous terrain by planting vines. To protect the vines from the sea breeze and salt spray, they excavated the lava and covered the landscape with tiny fields surrounded by dark basalt walls. These more or less regularly shaped currais or curraletas, as they're called, each enclose a dozen or so vines and create an extraordinary landscape inscribed as a UNESCO World Heritage site.

Grants are even provided for their maintenance, which is very labour-intensive and costly. The dark stone plays its part by storing heat during the day and releasing it at night, creating a unique microclimate.

In this distinctive *terroir*, the grapes mature quickly, ripening and drying on the vine.

There's no need to tie them up or raisin them in dryers in order to obtain straw wine. Before the grapes dry out, the winemakers pick and press the clusters to obtain very sweet juices, which mature into sweet wines. These wines have long been exported to make the island's fortune: the noblest tables in Europe, even the Russian tsars, appreciated the Verdelho dessert wine of Pico Island.

Around 1850, odium (powdery mildew) attacked the Azores. This fungal disease from America is caused by a white micro-organism. The vines withered and in the subsequent economic disaster people began to emigrate.

There are, however, chemical or biological solutions: sulphur spray, developed in the Languedoc in 1856 by Henri Marès, or the adoption of American vines that are resistant to the persistent enemy. Thus the Isabelle red grape variety was planted in the Azores before the disease could be brought under control.

Today, Terceira Island produces a sweet wine named Biscoitos after the planting holes dug into the lava, which are round like biscuits.

Local labels are *Verdelho des Açores* and *Terrantez*. *Lajido* is a sweet white from Pico Island. The hybrid grape Noah, which has long been banned in France, is fermented for local consumption.

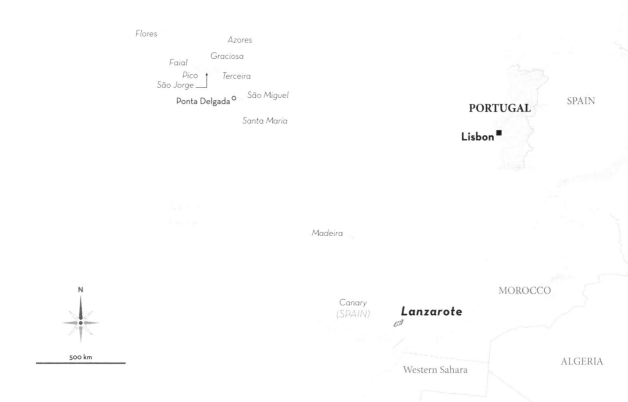

Flores

Azores

Faial   Graciosa

Pico   Terceira
São Jorge

Ponta Delgada°   São Miguel

Santa Maria

PORTUGAL   SPAIN

Lisbon■

Madeira

N

500 km

Canary   MOROCCO
(SPAIN)   **Lanzarote**

Western Sahara   ALGERIA

Wines of Lanzarote

Vines that can survive in a landscape of dark craters and no water

Lanzarote is a Spanish island in the Canary Islands off the African coast of Western Sahara. It has the worst possible conditions for agriculture: less than 200 mm of rainfall a year and very poor soil, partly covered in ash and scoria, and fragments of black volcanic rock. This volcano rock was expelled in 1730 when Timanfaya, the volcano that dominates the west of the island, erupted. The strong, hot winds of the Sahara also dry out any attempts at planting on the island.

Despite these difficult conditions, some winegrowers have tried the impossible by adapting to the local terrain. To the south of Arrecife, the island's capital, the La Geria vineyards are characterised by funnels (known locally as 'hoyos') several metres wide and ditches ('zanjas') that reach into the earth buried under the layer of ash.

This is where farmers planted vines, with their roots plunging deep into the subsoil. The sterile volcanic layer reduces evaporation and soaks up the meagre rainfall and night-time humidity, which it passes to the vines.

Low, half-moon-shaped lava walls also protect each vine from the drying winds. In a dark landscape, the deep green leaves of the vines are the only sign of plant life in these spectacular surroundings.

Another unique feature is that the insect known as phylloxera (Daktulosphaira vitifoliae), that ravages roots in other latitudes, hates volcanic soils. While the vines of Europe and the rest of the world fall victim to its proliferation, the vines of Lanzarote quietly continue to produce their grapes.

The El Grifo Museum of Wine Culture tells the story of this human adventure and displays ancient tools, even though the work and harvesting is still done by hand.

The local varieties of Malvasia, Muscat, Vijariego and Listán Negro, which can be tasted in the many bodegas along the scenic wine route, are unique.

SWITZERLAND

Milan

Venice

SLOVENIA

HUNGARY

CROATIA

FRANCE

BOSNIA AND
HERZEGOVINA

SERBIA

ITALY

MONTENEGRO

Kosovo

Rome

NORTH
MACEDONIA

Naples

Pompei

ALBANIA

GREECE

N

200 km

Wines of Pompeii

*Two thousand years after the tragedy,
Pompeii's vines reveal ancient techniques*

On 24 August in the year AD 79, there was a devastating eruption of Vesuvius. The delightful coastal town of Pompeii and the vineyards that had supplied the appreciative court of Rome were all preserved under the solidified ash. A longstanding viticultural tradition had been inherited from the Greeks; the frescoes unearthed by archaeologists show the importance accorded to the vines growing on the slopes of the volcano. The plain was used to grow food because, according to the Roman proverb, 'Bacchus loves the hills.' Vines, roots and stakes moulded in the ash have been excavated. These remarkable finds reveal the vine-training methods of the ancient world: the planting frame was 4 Roman feet square (1.18 x 1.18 metres) for vines worked by hand, larger for those where draft animals passed – as Pliny the Elder's *Historia Naturalis* (*Natural History*) confirms.

As land was scarce in the urban area, the Pompeian owners looked for high yields.

Planted in tight rows on the rich basalt soil, the vines provided dense vegetation and their shade kept down the weeds and hence the labour of removing them. So the vines had the soil's entire mineral and water reserves to themselves. The workers benefited from the shade too. The high pergolas (trellising) protected the grapes from ground predators, and the leaf canopy offered protection from the beady eyes of birds. These ingenious Romans optimised the yields of both labour and land.

The pergola wasn't the only vine-training system practised in antiquity. Pliny the Elder and the agronomist Columella cite five others: 'coverage', with stems laid on the ground, as in the cultivation of melons; the free-standing *gobelet* or bush vine system; the 'spindle' vertical cordon on trellising; the 'curtain' horizontal cordon supported by stakes, with a straight branch replacing the wire of trellised vines; and *alberate*, growing like a wild vine on a living tree, as still found near Naples with the Asprinio grape. The Romans, excellent winemakers that they were, adapted their vine training to different climates and terroirs. These six methods of cultivation can be seen in the vineyard of the Gallo-Roman Saint-Romain-en-Gal museum in Vienne (France). During the tragedy of Pompeii, Pliny became a victim of his own scientific curiosity, overcome by Vesuvius' sulphurous fumes.

Today, in the heart of the historic city, the Mastroberardino estate has planted 1.5 hectares with the local red varieties Piedirosso, Aglianico and Sciascinoso, close to the antiquities described by Pliny and depicted in frescoes. The only concessions to our age are that the plants are grafted onto American rootstock for fear of phylloxera. Mastroberardino stopped harvesting the Pompei vines in 2021, but continues to sell bottles of *Villa Dei Misteri* from previous vintages. Pergola cultivation has been partially replaced by poles, trellising or free-standing bushes so that the grapes ripen better.

The wine is made using modern methods. 'Otherwise it would be too rough to drink!' smiles the oenologist. The aim is twofold: to understand the old techniques and to disseminate the history of winemaking in the Campania region.

A bottle of *Villa dei misteri* (Villa of the Mysteries) red retails for about €100.

© Pierrick Bourgault

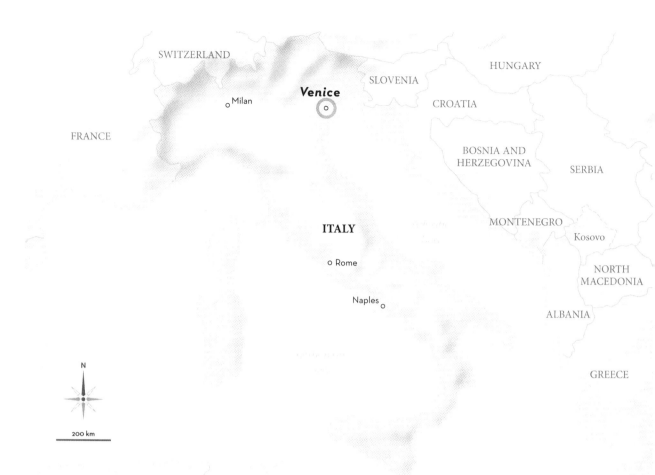

Wines of the Venetian lagoon

A salty terroir *by the sea*

Before Michel Thoulouze settled in Venice, he had launched television channels such as Planète, Canal Jimmy, CinéCinéma and Seasons. How has this audiovisual producer become a wine producer? 'I like to create things, change the landscape, starting from scratch. I'd never have bought an existing estate. My hobby has become my profession.'

The island of Sant'Erasmo is part of the municipality of Venice, but bears no resemblance to the city visited every year by 20 million tourists. When Thoulouze discovered some abandoned gardens by the sea, he consulted his winegrowing friends in Burgundy, who told him: 'Venice is an excellent marketing idea, but the wine must be good ...' But vines don't like salt.

Thoulouze settled there on a hunch. He came across a 17th-century map showing the location of a vineyard on his land. 'Soil analysis revealed traces of copper, meaning there must have been vines growing that were later abandoned, everything here being so difficult.'

This man didn't shrink from the difficulties – on the contrary. On the advice of Claude Bourguignon, a bioagriculturalist, he chose not to plough but to sow barley, Chinese radishes and sorghum for four years to prepare the soil. 'The neighbours were telling us we were crazy to plant vines without working the soil.' Next, with oenologist Alain Graillot of Crozes-Hermitage, he chose 'old white varieties that could have been planted at the time of the Venetian Republic: Istrian Malvasia, Vermentino and Fiano d'Avellino.'

Another unusual choice was to use own-root plants – i.e. not grafted onto American rootstock that is resistant to phylloxera – betting on the fact that the salinity would mitigate the aggressiveness of the parasite.

© G. Bombieri

Why take the risk of planting own-root vines? 'To recover the original taste of the wine,' says Thoulouze. 'The ungrafted plant is weird, it produces fewer grapes, some are large and others small, they grow like a bunch of adolescents, not all at the same rate. In the end, the wine is much better than expected. It hasn't much aroma but it's got plenty of body. Drink one glass and you want another. My wine is called Orto, which means garden, orchard.'

Bottling is done on a truck that arrives by boat – in Venice nothing is simple. Thoulouze gets around on an Ape (Italian for bee), the light three-wheeled vehicle that doesn't compact the soil, and he delivers by boat. His 4.5 hectares currently produce 10,000 bottles, soon to rise to 20,000. The mayor of Venice buys bottles as gifts for the city's guests.

As one of the neighbouring farmers says: 'This is the first time a wine of ours has been labelled!' Michel Thoulouze has earned the respect of his neighbours by his simple determination and, as he points out, 'the Italians have a culture of immigration'.

© G. Bombieri

CZECH REPUBLIC

GERMANY

SLOVAKIA

AUSTRIA

HUNGARY

SWITZERLAND

Vino della pace

SLOVENIA

FRANCE

o Milan

o Venice

CROATIA

BOSNIA AND
HERZEGOVINA

SERBIA

ITALY

MONTENEGRO

Kosovo

o Rome

o Naples

ALBANIA

GREEC

ALGERIA

N

TUNISIA

200 km

Il vino della pace : a 'peace wine' blended from 600 varieties from the five continents

'All the flavours of the Earth in a glass.'

The Friuli region of Italy, lying between Slovenia, the Alps and the Adriatic, is where Latin, Slavic and Germanic cultures intermingle, as shown on a map of grape varieties: the plantations of Merlot, Cabernet Franc, Pinot Blanc and Pinot Gris evoke the Napoleonic era and the years of French occupation, while the decorated barrels at the Cormons cooperative show that eastern Friuli was part of Austria until 1919.

The local varieties are so numerous (Verduzzo, Refosco, Picolit ...) that a grower has difficulty in choosing which to plant. This abundance complicates the work of wine experts, who need to know the varieties of the appellation zone and their specific problems, in particular phytosanitary requirements, in the absence of scientific studies. Biodiversity can also affect the marketing of a wine: how to explain to a potential buyer the differences in the characteristics of each vintage?

To overcome the problems posed by this diversity, the Friulians turned all this to their advantage and got their message across. Unlike the Italian tradition of naming a wine after its place of origin or *terroir*, Friuli labels indicate the grape variety. One of the specialities of the region's nurseries, at Rauscedo, has become the propagation of multiple varieties.

But the most spectacular initiative comes from the Cormons cooperative. Every year since 1983, its 200 members and international guests gather to harvest the 3-hectare heritage plot where 600 varieties from around the world have been planted: Syrah, Tulilah, Shurrebe, Pedral, Maizy, Marzemino, Terrano, Merlot, Gamay, Ucelut ... Pressed and fermented together, they produce a white 'peace wine', which brings together 'all the flavours of the Earth in a glass'.

These bottles with their artist's labels, packed in handsome wooden crates, are sent to embassies and heads of state around the world 'as a gift to promote friendship and good relations with Italy'.

Sinefinis: a political wine

*A wine from the Italy/Slovenia border is a reminder
that this was one land before Yugoslavia was created*

The wine known as *Sinefinis* means 'without end, without borders': aiming to symbolically reunite that same terroir separated just after the Second World War (Italy on one side and Yugoslavia on the other), it blends the production of a Slovenian and an Italian winemaker.

The land was even part of Austria until 1919, and then it was Italian until 1947 when the Iron Curtain came down. Producing the same local grape – known as Rumena Rebula or Ribolla Gialla depending on which side of the border it's grown – the Slovenian Matjaz Četrtič of the Ferdinand estate and the Italian Robert Princic da Giasbana of Gradis'ciutta have pooled their agricultural and commercial expertise, taken a Master's in the wine business and planned their Sinefinis wine. 'This transborder sparkling wine will of course be classified as a vin de table, but we'll explain our method on the label. The acidity of the Rebula is well suited to it.'

Although the basic wine is made at each vineyard, refining is a joint venture. This somewhat unlikely relationship aims to demonstrate that it is the same wineproducing region divided in two: the appellation is *Brda* in Slovenia and *Collio* in Italy. Wine can carry a political message too.

Geopolitics also dictated the choice of grape variety, explains Toni Gomiscek, director of Vinoteka Brda, the largest selection of wines in the zone. He sees this as an example of the absurd legacy of totalitarian regimes: 'In the Austro-Hungarian era, red wine was the priority because we were located in the south of the empire. That's normal: red is planted in the south. Then when we became Italians, we were obliged to plant white varieties. Logical: we'd become the north of the country!' The white Rebula grape is still grown there.

© Pierrick Bourgault

Vineyard music

'The vine whisperer'

A number of growers have installed loudspeakers in their vineyards. Among the best known is Giancarlo Cignozzi, of the Paradiso di Frassina estate in Tuscany (Italy).

This former lawyer has managed to convince Bose Corporation to provide enough speakers so that his estate is awash with sound. He broadcasts various genres of music over the seasons: sacred in winter, Baroque and Vivaldi in spring ...

Two researchers, Stefano Mancuso from the University of Florence, and Andrea Lucchi from the University of Pisa, are studying the effect on vine growth and insect infestations. The results are encouraging, both for promoting growth and for resistance to disease.

On the publicity front, Cignozzi has earned himself an international reputation. 'The vine whisperer' poetically compares the grape varieties to the different characters in Mozart operas: brought together in a blend, these grapes/characters all have their role to play.

The music plays on an endless loop in the vineyards that produce the *Flauto Magico* (Magic Flute) vintage. 'An austere wine but with soft and elegant tannins ... Thanks to Amadeus? I think so – but you be the judge!' One of his labels depicts the grapes as so many notes on a stave. Another of his wines, *12 UVE*, associates twelve varieties with the twelve notes of the chromatic scale.

Other French wineries are also experimenting with music. The Génodics company cites over 200 installations in vineyards, market gardens and farms where sound waves are used for therapeutic purposes. Physicist Joël Sternheimer has observed that the biosynthesis of the proteins that make up every living being is associated with frequencies and rhythms, which he calls *protéodies* ('protein melodies'). A sound sequence could act on this synthesis, stimulate or inhibit an amino acid, regulate biological processes, strengthen natural resistance, and treat viral, bacterial or fungal diseases. According to Michel Loriot, president of Vignerons Indépendants de Champagne: 'Music for plants broadcast through my vines gives the grapes better resistance to disease and allows them to thrive.' Esca, the devastating fungus that attacks the woody stems of the vines, also seems to be held at bay with this treatment.

alparadisodifrassina.it

Music in the cellars

Michel Loriot also practises music therapy in his cellars: 'The greatest composers nurture the bottled wines: they ferment for two months to the strains of Beethoven's *Pastoral Symphony*. Then Mozart, Brahms, Mahler, Vivaldi and Elgar turn up to join in the magic of effervescence. The vibrations of the notes reach the wine, its yeasts and proteins. They affect its structure and help to bring out all its flavours and aromas during the ageing process.'

Biodynamic winemaker Nicolas Joly uses a minimalist technique: 'It's better to strike a single note with a tuning fork in the tank.'

Some winemakers also play the violin or accordion to their casks or sound a hunting horn on the slopes.

champagne-michelloriot.com

The effect of music at tastings

Music also alters our intellectual perception and influences our sense of taste. Ophelia Deroy, researcher at the Centre for the Study of the Senses at the University of London, describes such an experiment: 'Participants who were tasting wines to the voices of *Carmina Burana* judged these wines to be more characterful than did those people who were tasting them to the accompaniment of other music. Conversely, the wines were judged more dynamic and refreshing when served in a room where Depeche Mode's *Just Can't Get Enough* – itself fresh and dynamic – was playing.'

But don't overdo it: stimulating too many senses at once (taste, vision, hearing ...) may ruin your concentration and the perception that a tasting session demands. Serving wine against a background of images and sounds may overwhelm the target audience with too much information, or even prejudge the outcome.

Plenty of festivals associate music with wine. Some music-loving winetasters recommend a particular track to accompany a certain bottle. This is often personal taste, but the analogy between the sensations of hearing and drinking can sometimes be expressed in eloquent terms. A notable example being the *sonorités aromatiques* ('aromatic tones') of Frédéric Beneix and Marien Nègre of Wine4Melomanes, Château La Croix du Merle (SaintÉmilion). The estate also plays music in its vineyards and winery.

Disturbing links between music and vines

In their vocabulary, tasters distinguish notes (woody, spicy ...), evoking the opening, finish and harmony, the range of the wines. They estimate a wine's finish by the number of seconds (caudalie)* a sensation persists in the mouth – the silence after Mozart is still Mozart. The shape of a glass and the acoustics of a concert hall are comparable, as these two spaces can enhance or disturb the work of the winemaker as conductor.

For thousands of years grapes have been trodden by foot, with or without boots, to the rhythm of work songs accompanying the winery tasks. In France, this habit of singing at work died out after the 1914–18 war. The wine reserved for Mass was accompanied by hymns, while banquets resounded to drinking songs.

'The score is written on the ground,' used to say Jacques Puisais, oenologist and philosopher, founder of the French Institut du Goût (association dedicated to an appreciation of taste). As a visual analogy: along the rows of vines, the training wires look like a musical score on which the clusters of grapes hang like notes.

Sparkling wine is the most voluble. Uncorking a bottle is the opportunity for an explosive sound, which sophisticated hosts avoid because they prefer the discreet murmur of bubbles. The sound of a cork popping is still the finest argument in favour of traditional corks rather than aluminium caps.

SWITZERLAND

HUNGARY

SLOVENIA

Milan

CROATIA

Venice

FRANCE

BOSNIA AND
HERZEGOVINA

SERBIA

ITALY

MONTENEGRO

Kosovo

Rome

NORTH
MACEDONIA

Naples

ALBANIA

N

GREECE

200 km

Pantelleria

The alberello vines of Pantelleria

The first traditional vinegrowing practice to be listed by UNESCO

In late November 2014, the representatives of 161 states voted unanimously to register the cultivation of bush vines trained low on the ground with no trellising (vite ad alberello) on the Mediterranean island of Pantelleria as Intangible Cultural Heritage. This UNESCO list of local traditions, festivals and performances is now open to outstanding agricultural practices.

The 8,300-hectare Italian island of Pantelleria, which is closer to Tunisia (72 kilometres) than it is to Sicily (100 kilometres), has been transformed into a garden paradise over centuries of hard work by the inhabitants. On this virtually uncultivable land, studded with volcanic rocks, successive generations have built thousands of kilometres of retaining walls with little terraces where a few vines or caper shrubs grow. The island resembles an ancient city where only the walls are left standing.

The challenge was enormous: no rain (barely 300 millimetres, almost exclusively in winter), and a burning, sand-laden wind (the sirocco) that dries up the foliage, disrupts flowering and fertilisation and damages the fruit when it does grow.

Under this African sun there are no sources of fresh water, just sulphurous volcanic springs that are full of minerals, thermal, undrinkable. Impossible to irrigate. In case of fire there's only seawater, which would damage the crops.

Passerillage (drying grapes on the vine) at Carole Bouquet's

Drying grapes on the De Bartoli estate

For centuries the island was also prey to pirates because of its strategic position.

The islanders survived by building Mediterranean-style houses known as *dammusi*. Their domed roof terraces catch the winter rainfall and the water is stored in underground cisterns. Traditionally, the narrow windows gave protection from the wind and any marauders; at night, the shutters hid the glow of the lights inside.

Walls that are constantly repaired and extended supported the small gardens.

Towers several metres high, known as 'Arab gardens', were built to protect each orange tree, each lemon tree, from the wind. Pantelleria really does raise its fruit trees with the same care as livestock for an agricultural show: the sloping tops of the walls direct the least drop of rain inside the garden.

At Pantelleria, the plants have lost the habit of taking in water through their roots. They absorb it through their leaves, from the condensation caused by the temperature difference between night and day in the humid marine climate. This phenomenon occurs inside the high walls of the Arab gardens, as well as in every hollow dug out to plant a vine, pruned *ad alberello* (goblet), whose stems creep along the ground. This humble *alberello* technique, the symbol of a cultivation system that is as laborious as it is ingenious, is now part of the Intangible Cultural Heritage of humanity.

For centuries the farmers cultivated grapes in order to export raisins. Now they produce *Passito di Pantelleria*, a naturally sweet white wine paradoxically flowing from such a harsh island, and a dry white. Passito is obtained by adding raisins to the fermenting juice, as in Hungary's *Tokaji Aszú*.

Pantelleria, a rural community on the fringes of Africa, is now a resort for jet-set socialites: Carole Bouquet has bought an estate and produces the *Sangue d'oro* label; Gérard Depardieu has lived there; Giorgio Armani, Sting and Madonna like to visit. The new UNESCO status will enhance the reputation of the island's wines.

© Pierrick Bourgault

Preparing Passito, Donnafugata estate

Jack and the beanstalk vines

These 15-metre vines attach themselves to poplar trees,
as they have done since antiquity

Vines are creepers that naturally grow up towards the sun. As Pliny the Elder explains in his *Natural History*, the Romans let them climb trees, which cut out the need to install stakes while distancing the grapes from the humidity and predators at ground level.

Of course, harvesting in the treetops was risky and the workers stipulated that, if they fell, they would be 'burned and buried at the owner's expense'.

In his 1600 work *The Theatre of Agriculture and Husbandry Fields*, Olivier de Serres also describes vines clinging to tall trees: 'These vines *en hautain* (at great height) were developed in France mainly in Brie, Champagne, Burgundy, Berry and other provinces,' i.e. mainly in the north, where sunshine is sometimes lacking and humidity is high. Today, a few particularly high vines persist in Italy, Crete and Portugal. Those of the celebrated *vinho verde* grow along the roadsides and in gardens. Between the rows, which were about 15 metres apart, the farmers grew wheat, hemp or vegetables, a combination of different species that is known as interplanting. This ancient method of cultivation, which uses little ground space but is labour intensive, has almost completely disappeared.

Portuguese *vinho verde* now uses trellised vines so that the training and harvesting are easier to mechanise.

In Campania (Italy), some estates still make wine from hundred-year-old non-grafted vines that have resisted phylloxera. This rootstock of the white Asprinio ('bitter') grape climbs poplars because the tree grows fast, straight up towards the light, and its small leaves let the vine take advantage of the sunshine. Another height-related advantage: the wind from the nearby Mediterranean dries out any moisture and prevents the grapes from developing fungal diseases.

The Numeroso family, owner of the Borboni estate, has some of these giant vines near Aversa (Campania). As they stand almost 15 metres tall, they're neither pruned nor treated. To harvest these spectacular green walls laden with grapes, the workers climb ladders (each has their own, adapted to their size and shape) and fill small pointed baskets called *fascine*, which sink into the ground when dropped. An assistant empties out the grapes and the baskets are pulled up again by rope, like groceries in Naples. 'But young people no longer want to work this way,' you'll hear. 'My youngest picker is 60,' sighs Mario Caputo, another winemaker.

Each vine yields a large quantity of not very ripe grapes that are still acidic – characteristic of the Asprinio d'Aversa appellation. Several wineries make good use of this acidity, producing a sparkling wine by the traditional (champagne) bottled method or in a classic closed tank.

Paradoxically, Numeroso also turns this variety of grape into its polar opposite – dessert wine. To achieve this curiosity, he harvests in October, dries the grapes under cover and presses them in January: 'I wanted to bring back a childhood memory. After the harvest, my parents kept a few branches and we ate grapes at Christmas. They also pressed them to make a sweet wine.'

The strongest wine in the world

Superprimitivo, *produced under the sun of the Ionian Sea,*
is notable for its extraordinary alcohol level of 19.5 per cent.

The juice of ripe grapes contains sugars that feed the yeasts (fungal spores naturally present on the leaves and in the cellar that will cause fermentation), which release alcohol and carbon dioxide. Their feast ends when there's no more sugar to consume, or if the strength of the alcohol kills the yeasts themselves: about 18 per cent appears to be the maximum level they can survive.

For this reason, wines over 18 per cent are usually obtained by adding distilled alcohol, during or after fermentation: these are called fortified wines. Note that there is no upper limit to the level of alcohol in wine (Guido Baldeschi, Oenology Commission, International Organisation of Vine and Wine).

There are rare exceptions, however. In the southern Italian region of Puglia, where the sun beats down relentlessly, the Primitivo grape (the name means 'early') matures quickly: harvest begins in late August. If delayed, the sugars concentrate in the overripe grapes and the yeasts feast.

In the region of Puglia, at Acquaviva delle Fonti near the city of Bari, the Chiaromonte family sells a Muro Sant'Angelo cuvée at 16.5% and its riserva at 18%. The Selezione Chiaromonte proudly displays its 19% alcohol content. This type of titration is not uncommon in the appellation.

The biological activity of yeast continues at such high levels of alcohol because there are 'local yeasts that can convert sugar in these extreme conditions'.

In fact, the yeasts don't consume all the sugar: 5–10 grams per litre remain after fermentation, which rounds out the flavours in the style of New World wines. A few months after the harvest, these wines are ready to drink and give off notes of black fruits, preserved plums, cherries in eau-de-vie, dried figs, carob, liquorice, tobacco, chocolate and jam ... while keeping the vivacity and freshness of their youth.

High alcohol levels: pros and cons

Competition judges tend to reward expressive wines, whether for their aroma or their flavour. Alcohol tends to lift the taste. The US wine critic Robert Parker's ratings on a 100-point scale favour wines with high alcohol content, a style that's been followed by winemakers worldwide.

In France too, in the southern vineyards of Rhône and Languedoc, the alcohol level is high: whereas there used to be a market for large quantities of wine, now quality wines in smaller quantities are sought after. So winemakers limit their output, carrying out a green harvest in June to eliminate some of the grape clusters so that the remainder can benefit from all the sap of the vine and reach perfect maturity. Thanks to localised, very accurate online weather forecasts, growers are harvesting later, so the grapes are riper.

Climate change is also playing a role in increased alcohol levels.

The limits are both fiscal and psychological. Nicola Chiaromonte exports his wines from Puglia to Asia and the USA, but not to the UK or Sweden where alcohol is heavily taxed. A number of restaurant customers are concerned about drinking wine at 14.5 per cent and prefer to order 13 per cent, even if the difference seems insignificant.

The vineyard of pencils

An explosion of colours just a stone's throw from the Langhe

Piercarlo Anfosso had a problem: the workers from the cooperatives who came to help him in the vineyards could never understand where his property ended and where his neighbours' properties began. He decided to fix that by painting the posts that marked the boundaries of his land red. They stood out so beautifully in the middle of the vineyard that Piercarlo decided in the off-season to paint all the other posts a different shade and chisel them into the shape of magnificent, coloured pencils.

This is how the Vigna dei Pastelli ('vineyard of pencils') was born. Marked out by a line of giant, colourful pencils that point to the beginning of each row and bring a splash of bright, pretty colours in a place drowned by the green of the vines, the vineyard offers a breathtaking view that, on a clear day, stretches all the way to Mount Viso.

The concept quickly caught on, and Piercarlo became so well known in the Asti region that he was able to organise tastings and parties on his splendid hillside vineyards. A wedding was even celebrated in the wonderful surroundings.

The estate is on the border between the provinces of Asti and Cuneo, in an area dominated by vineyards, with rows of vines stretching across the gentle hills. Piercarlo produces an excellent Barbera, an incredible Dolcetto and a Muscat that has won several awards at the Asti Douja d'Or national wine competition: the fabulous Moscato d'Asti DOCG I Pastelli.

Just 150 metres from the Pastelli hill is the colourful little church of the Beata vergine del Carmine (Blessed Virgin of Carmine), built in the 18th century in the middle of the countryside and repainted in 2017 by the British artist David Tremlett using the wall-drawing technique. The area has been opened up to artists to add splashes of bright colour to the greenery.

SWITZERLAND

FRANCE

o Milan

o Venice

SLOVENIA

HUNGARY

CROATIA

BOSNIA AND
HERZEGOVINA

SERBIA

Fuori Marmo

ITALY

o Rome

o Naples

MONTENEGRO

Kosovo

NORTH
MACEDONIA

ALBANIA

GREECE

N

200 km

Fuori Marmo

A Tuscan cuvée matured in Carrara white marble jars

The white marble of Carrara, in Tuscany, is famous for its aesthetic quality and its translucent and sensuous appearance which has made it much appreciated by sculptors such as Michelangelo.

Historically, it was also used to store, in a brine of aromatic herbs, the lard from pigs slaughtered in the autumn. After a few months of maturing, at the end of winter, this unearthed lardo di colonnata represented a delicious, melt-in-the-mouth and delicate food that gave the quarry workers the energy they needed to cut and move blocks of marble.

Meanwhile, wine was fermented in vats carved from the local stone and stored in the cellars. Of course, in the open air, oxidation and fermentation gradually transformed it into vinegar. Only the corked amphorae or light barrels used by Celtic craftsmen made it possible to keep wine longer.

While preserving wine in stone is nothing new (in fact, it's a return to original winemaking methods), carving egg-shaped marble jars to mature wine in is an original idea. Three-star Michelin chef Yannick Alléno suggested it to winemaker Olivier Paul-Morandini of the Fuori Mondo Domaine, in the Maremma hills of Tuscany.

This is how Fuori Marmo ('out of marble') was born. It is the first wine to be matured in Carrara marble jars. Using a 34.8-tonne block of white Seravezza marble, sculptor Paolo Carli spent five months shaping two 17.5-hectolitre (1.75 cubic metre) ovoid amphorae, each weighing two tonnes.

Olivier Paul-Morandini then studied the interactions with the wine. The marble's calcium carbonate reduces the acidity of the wine and is even an authorised additive in oenology.

Two and a half years of fine-tuning later, the cuvée was finally unveiled: a 2019 Cabernet Sauvignon IGT Costa Toscana. The thick white paper label imitates the relief of a mysterious parietal sculpture, and the 75-centilitre bottles sell for more than €1,000 each.

Before Fuori Marmo, other attempts were made to age wine in stone, in Italy and at the Austrian Wachau estate. One example is Steinwerk, made from the white Grüner Veltliner grape, which sells for around €20 a bottle and is fermented and matured in vats of local marble and granite.

Verjuice

Can late-ripening grapes be used to make wine?

Verjuice ('green juice') is a tangy liquid that was widely used in medieval cooking. It is obtained by pressing various plants (sorrel, wild fruits ...) and most often unripe grapes, especially those small clusters that are still green in autumn and that the winemakers called verjus. As fruit with little or no sugars (such as unripe grapes) cannot feed the yeasts that convert sugar into alcohol, it is theoretically impossible to obtain an alcoholic brew, or wine, from verjuice.

However, in the vineyards of Puglia, in southern Italy, the sun is so intense that late clusters of green grapes finally begin to ripen. Although the typical harvest normally begins in August, a second harvest in late October collects these almost sweet grapes. The winemaker takes advantage of their acidity to create fresh wines, particularly spumante.

Filippo Cassano, of Puglia's Polvanera estate, produces a sparkling rosé under the label *Metodo classico* from his Primitivo vines. Following the same method of fermentation in bottles as used for champagne, he adds 8 grams of sugar per litre to the dosage liquor, to sweeten the '*rosé brut*'. One of his neighbours, Nicola Chiaromonte, also harvests again in October for verjuice.

© Pierrick Bourgault

Although the use of acidic flavours in the kitchen has greatly diminished since the Middle Ages, it lingers on in recipes such as tête de veau vinaigrette (slowcooked calf's head) or in the delightful southern Italian habit of squeezing a lemon over grilled meat. Of course, in the old days cooks used only local ingredients and a great many of them didn't even know that lemons existed.

Acidic juices are also used to deglaze meat pans after cooking. Sometimes mould appeared, so medieval cooks had to salt the verjuice to conserve it and discourage bacteria. The acidic taste of verjuice is nothing like that of vinegar, which is obtained after oxidation of the alcohol from wine or cider by acetic acid bacteria.

A sparkling wine to disgorge at home

Disgorgement Slovenian style

The 'traditional' or '*champenoise*' method (but this term is banned on labels) for the preparation of sparkling wines causes secondary fermentation inside the bottle by the addition of sugar and yeast.

Forced to remain in the bottle, which is closed by a solid cork, the carbon dioxide generated by the fermentation process dissolves into the wine – hence the bubbles. After this second fermentation, a deposit of dead yeast falls to the bottom of the bottle – rather unattractive for a wine that is meant to embody elegance!

So champagne makers have found a solution: they store the bottles neck down and the yeast falls onto the cap. Disgorgement involves opening each bottle with a special tool, the slug of yeast coming away with each cap. As some liquid has been lost during the operation, the bottle is topped up with a little wine, perhaps a sweet one (*liqueur d'expédition*), the bottle is resealed … et voilà!

Manual disgorgement ('on the fly') used to be a spectacular operation. Nowadays, however, it takes place in a machine that freezes the neck of the bottle.

In Slovenia, winemaker Ales Kristančič of the Movia (Dobrovo) estate is betting that he can trust sommeliers or knowledgeable consumers to carry out this technical step and sell a wine that needs to be disgorged before drinking. 'This is the only part of the process that we can outsource and which will go some way to explaining sparkling wines,' says Kristančič, heir to a long line of winemakers. In the former Yugoslavia, Marshal Tito himself appreciated this winery and spared it from nationalisation, he adds.

Kristančič is also quite the comedian, as free-thinking as he seems to be self-taught, and sets the scene with coloured lights. 'Watch out, always keep the bottle neck pointing downwards. We'll stick the new label on upside down, to remind people how to store our bottles.'

Isn't it awkward to impose such constraints on the customer? 'Not at all, sommeliers love it – adds to their value!' Rather like bartenders mixing cocktails. To help them, Kristančič provides a special key or a transparent ice bucket with a bottle opener in the base.

His Puro blend is original in another way too: 'Unlike the traditional method, no sugar is added, nor any yeast to encourage fermentation in the bottle: only the must with its own sugar and micro-organisms, which you disgorge yourself when you open the bottle. So the wine continues to develop with its natural yeasts until it is drunk, and contains no sulphites. It has an infinite life. *Puro* is a very special sparkling wine!'

But beware: this living bottle must be kept cool. Any rise in temperature may stimulate the yeast, with explosive results.

© Pierrick Bourgault

ROMANIA

SERBIA

BULGARIA

Sofia

KOSOVO

Plovdiv

Skopje

NORTH
MACEDONIA

Thessaloniki

ALBANIA

Thassos

*Halkidiki
peninsula*

Karies

Çanakkale

Lemnos

GREECE

TURKEY

*Northern
Sporades*

Eubea

Rouvalis

Athens

N

100 km

Greek rosé from the Rouvalis estate

A rosé that defies the regulations by blending red and white grapes

What is rosé wine? A mixture of white and red? The question was raised in 2009 when certain enterprises, notably in Australia and South Africa, made the decision to combine these two colours to conquer the expanding rosé market. Led by Provence in the south of France, Old World winemakers saw red: if rosé was indeed a white with a few drops of added colour, it would taste like white, so it's not just the colour that makes the wine pink.

White wine is the juice of white grapes (or red grapes yielding white juice) pressed soon after harvest and left to ferment. Red wine, on the other hand, comes from grapes that have been macerated and fermented from one to several weeks, with their skins and seeds, before pressing. During this phase, the skins and seeds give the juice colour, flavour and tannins as the developing alcohol extracts various aromatic compounds.

The rosé technique falls between the two: red grapes with white juice macerate for several hours without fermenting, and this contact with the skins lightly colours the juice. After pressing, the coloured grape juice is fermented. The water of grape juice (in rosé wine) or the alcohol produced by fermentation (in red wine) does not extract the same molecules.

A disturbing discovery was made at the Oenoforos estate belonging to Angelos Rouvalis, former vice-president of the Greek Wine Federation: 75–85 per cent Syrah (red) and 25–15 per cent Viognier (white) on a rosé specification sheet. 'The aromas of red fruit and violet come from the Syrah, those of apple, passion fruit and grapefruit from the Viognier.' The taste is nothing if not expressive, somewhere between bananas and boiled sweets.

In theory, mixing white and red wine is banned. At Oenoforos, two colours of grape are mixed for four to eight hours and then pressed.

The juice of the two varieties is fermented at a low temperature (12 °C) for a fortnight or so.

So what the Greeks have devised is a rosé version of *Côte-rôtie*, one of the most prestigious Côtes du Rhône, which also blends Syrah with Viognier to make a fullbodied red.

White and red grape blends are rare

Blending of different coloured grapes is the exception rather than the rule. In Tuscany, the chianti regulations allow bunches of white grapes to be added to fermentation tanks to soften the reds, but the wine is still red. Bordeaux winemakers used to add some local white grapes to their claret for the same reason. In Provence, the Luberon appellation allows up to 20% of white grapes, such as Vermentino, to be added to its red grapes, before fermentation of course. This is not because of the colour of the rosé, but because vermentino is an aromatic grape variety. Today, this white wine is in demand, so it is vinified as white and rarely blended with black grapes to produce red or rosé.

The first wines were light in colour

Ancient Greece contributed greatly to the spread of winemaking skills by teaching the Etruscans of pre-Roman Italy, who in their turn passed their skills on to the Roman colonisers of Europe. Archaeological ruins, writings, and decorations on pottery all show that the first wines were light-coloured. The grapes crushed underfoot in a *palmento* (cistern), and the juice that was immediately stored for fermentation, could only have produced a white or a rosé. Red wine came later, when the dark skins had been left to macerate

© Pierrick Bourgault

135

Novorossiysk

RUSSIA

Pyatigorsk

Sochi

5 642 m

Sukhumi

Caucasus

North
Ossetia

5 203 m

Vladikavkaz

Grozznyy

Abkhazia

Mou

5 047 m

n

t

South Ossetia
Tskhinvali

a

i

n

s

Poti

Gori

GEORGIA

Tbilisi

Kakheti

N

Batumi

Artvin

200 km

TURKEY

ARMENIA

AZERBAIJAN

Yerevan

The amphora wines of Georgia

Wines in giant amphorae have retained the flavours of antiquity

Georgia, with Russia to the north and Turkey to the south, has seen many waves of invaders over the centuries. So the farmers of this fertile land, with its temperate climate, have long been in the habit of hiding their wine, oil and cereals in amphorae, buried out of sight. Examples of this pottery, known as *kvevri* ('large jar'), containing an orange wine that is still drinkable despite its acidity and slightly vinegary taste, are sometimes excavated.

Under communism, Georgia's wine-producing reputation led to the construction of manufacturing plants whose wine was exported throughout the Soviet empire. But rural and townspeople alike continued to harvest the vines from their gardens and prepare their family wine in amphorae.

The recipe is simple, as explained by grower Tamasi Natroshvili: 'We tread the grape clusters, then put them to ferment in amphorae. We stir the mix with a stick. After twenty to twenty-five days, when the marc (skins and stem) has sunk to the bottom, we transfer the wine to another amphora. A wicker basket is used as a filter. We distil the marc and the small stems to obtain an alcohol called *tchatcha*. Two weeks later, we transfer the wine to yet another amphora and cork it tightly. Three decantings follow: in spring; for the Transfiguration of Christ festival (6 August); and for the new harvests. For successful storage the amphorae must always be full of wine.'

This *kakhetian* method (named after Georgia's premier wine-producing region of Kakheti, pronounced *careti*) requires no running water, electricity, barrels, temperature control or winepress: just a stick, a basket and some amphorae.

The wines made by the *imerouli* method (from the Imereti region) are less harsh because the grapes are hand-separated from the stems that would spoil the taste. The winemaking process is identical for both red and white grapes. It's also a fascinating journey back in time, throwing light on the methods of antiquity.

Today, this ancient and rustic wine, with its marked acidity, is popular with lovers of natural wine, and cellars with buried amphorae are being built. Unfortunately it's difficult to find potters to make these vessels, which can contain from 1 to 3 tonnes of wine. The ancient amphorae are porous, dirty and often damaged, so restoring them is difficult.

Where can Georgian amphorae wines be found?

Several wines produced in Georgia are fermented in amphorae: *Clos des amandiers*, *Our Wine*, from Soliko Tsaishvili, Zurab Topuridze and Iago Bitarishvili.

triplea.it

Amphorae unearthed

Amphorae buried up to their necks, out of sight and out of mind

Iraq's clandestine wines

*In Kurdistan, a few growers discreetly strive to cultivate
vines and make wine*

Is viniculture disappearing from the land of Mesopotamia, where it was developed? Paradoxically, it isn't Islam that destroyed the wine industry in Iraq, but Saddam Hussein, a secular wine lover whose taste for Mateus, a sparkling Portuguese rosé found in the cellars of his palace, was well known. The genocide he perpetrated in Kurdistan from 1987 to 1991 and the ensuing population exodus meant that the vineyards were abandoned.

The terrorism born of war is now sufficiently menacing to force growers underground. Discretion is the rule when it comes to alcoholic beverages. With no promotion and no phylloxera, local varieties and wild vines cling to the hillsides. The presence of well-maintained rootstock and plots that have been recently planted with prunings suggests that the growers are resisting – second nature to the Kurds.

The grape varieties sold in Kurdistan's markets or by the roadside are black (Mermerk, Rosh Mew), red (Taefi, Kamali), yellow (Zarek, Hejaze, Khateni, Keshmesh) or red and white (Helwani). 'With these grapes, we can do anything,' explains a stallholder. 'Table grapes, raisins, juice, wine, arak, vinegar!' The conversation naturally veers towards the fermentation process. 'Here, twenty-five years before Saddam Hussein flattened the villages, we made wine and arak.' And now? 'We still do it!' exclaims a neighbour.

In a Christian village near Amadiya, the vines grow vigorously around the church to form hedges and pergolas. A thick non-grafted root, 30 centimetres in diameter, feeds a vast canopy of leaves and clusters of grapes. Its owner describes the production of arak: 'I harvest the grapes, crush them and leave them in a tank for seven days before distilling to get a grape alcohol of about 70 degrees.' He responds to a request to visit his set-up with a smile: 'We haven't made any for years!'

At the corner shop, a man sipping tea with friends sells his own wine in recycled bottles: '€7 for the good one, less for the other.' This fruity wine, fermented a few weeks earlier, is already oxidised. 'I crush Mermek grapes in a vat. After seven days of fermentation, I bottle the juice. I produce a few hundred bottles a year.'

His childhood memories are of villagers making their wine in earthenware jars. He says he bought a still in Baghdad but now it's nowhere to be seen. 'It's in a nearby village; anyway we don't use it much any more ...'. He too refers to himself as an 'Assyrian Christian'.

The bishop of Dohuk, Monsignor Rabban, opened a secular free school for boys and girls, both Muslims and Christians. This even-handed diplomat, respected by all, refuses to reveal the source of communion wine in his diocese, presumably to protect his winemaker friends. The secret is as well guarded as if it had been heard in the confessional.

In the mountains near the Turkish border, a church supplier agrees to testify on condition that his name isn't mentioned and no pictures taken in which he might be recognised.

His village is sited near the snowy peaks where several hundred thousand Kurds fled during the winter of 1991; no house was left standing after the passage of Saddam Hussein's troops, as in almost all of Kurdistan. Now, the people are rebuilding with reinforced concrete and the vines are growing again, spilling over the walls of the Christian cemetery beside the church, forming hedges and invading the village, a witness to the intense wine-producing activities of the past. Rainfall is 800–1,000 millimetres a year, altitude 800 metres, with brilliant sunshine.

© Pierrick Bourgault

Wines of the Gobi desert (China)

How can wine be made in a land frozen in winter,
torrid in summer and with never a drop of rain?

Nothing predisposes western China, on the Mongolian border, to the cultivation of vines. Over 2,500 kilometres from the sea, this is the most continental region in the world: in winter, with temperatures between –20 °C and –30 °C, plants completely freeze.

These obstacles weren't enough to deter the Chinese: in 1949, when Peking annexed Turkestan, which is two and a half times the size of France, an ancient irrigation system brought water from the Tian Shan mountains to the oases of the Silk Road. The Uighurs had cultivated vines for centuries to produce raisins.

So Peking named this region Xinjiang (New Frontier) and from 1980 decided to plant thousands of hectares with Western grape varieties (Cabernet Sauvignon, Syrah, Merlot, Chardonnay, Chenin Blanc, Riesling ...) as well as local varieties (Beichun, Cibayi, Shabulawe ...). In eastern China, the land in provinces such as Shandong is expensive, criss-crossed with road networks and conurbations, and polluted by industry.

So that vines will flourish in the former desert, the ditches between the rows are flooded six to ten times a year. 'Here, no rain, so no diseases, treatments, copper, or sulphur!' assures Grégory Michel, who has run part of the Lulan estate organically until 2020. These 90 hectares, an area similar to the largest European vineyards, produce an amazing local Muscat, *Rou Ding Xiang*, which is naturally sweet when fermented and popular with the Japanese. Their top-of-the-range wines, packaged like precious perfumes, sell for €150 a bottle.

◀ Plain after earthing-up

Citic Guo'An wineries

But how to protect the rootstock from frost? On winter evenings, the market gardeners of Xinjiang cover their greenhouses with thick quilting; or sometimes blankets packed around the vines does the trick. In the Gobi desert, as soon as the September harvest is over, the farmers and migrant workers waste no time in pruning the vines, bending over the stems and burying them in furrows that they protect by covering with soil. By late October, the earthing-up has erased all sign of vegetation from the landscape. Over tens of thousands of hectares, there is just the plain bristling with bare stakes. In spring, the plentiful labour force arrives to unearth the vines, tie them up again and regrowth begins – always with the risk of a late frost.

On its 10,000 hectares, Citic Guo'An wineries produce a rosé from the Syrah grape, *Suntime Yili River*. Paradoxically, this Chinese wine isn't sold in China because, as confirmed by Yiran Liu, director of the Maison du Languedoc-Roussillon in Shanghai, 'The Chinese market isn't ready for rosé. Men don't order it because they consider it a women's drink.' Citic Guo'An has also created a Riesling-based Sushi Time wine to accompany Japanese restaurant specialities, which is also exported.

© Pierrick Bourgault

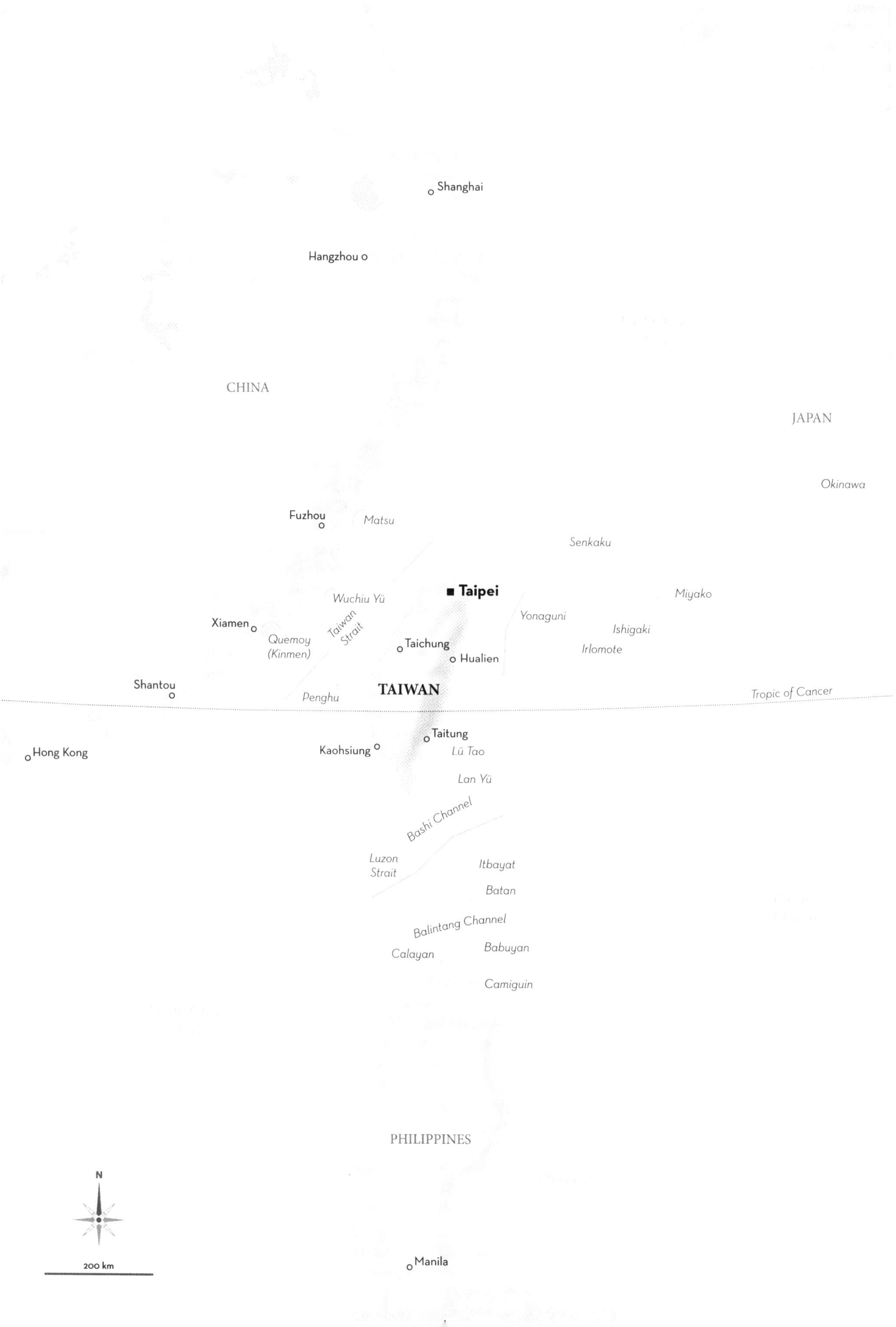

Shanghai

Hangzhou

CHINA

JAPAN

Okinawa

Fuzhou
Matsu

Senkaku

■ **Taipei**

Miyako

Wuchiu Yü

Yonaguni

Xiamen
Quemoy
(Kinmen)

Taiwan Strait

Taichung

Ishigaki

Irlomote

Hualien

Shantou

TAIWAN

Penghu

Tropic of Cancer

Hong Kong

Kaohsiung

Taitung

Lü Tao

Lan Yü

Bashi Channel

Luzon Strait

Itbayat

Batan

Balintang Channel

Calayan

Babuyan

Camiguin

PHILIPPINES

N

200 km

Manila

Taiwan's double harvests

On this tropical island, two or three harvests
a year give huge yields

'All seasons are good for growing grapes here,' smiles Chen Ching Fung. 'In France, you only have one!' The owner of a small theme park inspired by the world of wine, the Railway Valley Winery, he tells the story of the vineyard's year: 'We cut back the vines in February–March, then the vine buds and leaves appear. We harvest in early July and immediately do a new cutback, leaving no green leaves on the stem. A second growing cycle begins, ending with a second harvest in November or December.' For three annual cycles – and this practice concerns table grapes in particular – the vines will be cultivated under glass, even lit up at night, sometimes blitzed by irrigating them with salt water to stimulate fruiting. The only drawback of the climate is 'typhoons that are more dangerous than insects and diseases', according to Hong Ji-Bei, grower at Tai Chung, in the centre west of the island on Shu Sheug estate. The vines aren't cultivated on trellises but on pergolas, which are more resistant to cyclones.

In Taiwan, the vineyards alternate with flooded rice fields and high-tech factories. On this island four times the size of Corsica, with a population density a hundred times greater, production is paramount. At about €500,000 a hectare, the land has to be as profitable as possible and the growers fertilise it heavily. Chang Shu-Gen, owner of the Song-He estate at Tai Chung, sprays three times: 'potassium and nitrogen at pruning time and again when the grapes are half ripe; phosphorus before the harvest to harden the skins, discourage mildew and insect damage, together with animal waste, crushed seaweed and oysters.' The winemakers even grow cabbages between the rows. Not a square metre is left bare.

Chen Ching Fung claims he produces 700 quintals of grapes per hectare (i.e. 7 kilos per square metre!) and some growers more than double that – ten times more than in Europe. The yields are so high that, even under the tropical climate, they have to add sugar before and after fermentation. 'Because the customers like sweet wine,' the grower justifies himself, choosing Japanese yeasts 'to produce wine with the taste of oxidation and honey.' Of course, Chen Ching Fung exports to Japan, the former colonising country. Particular attention is paid to the labels and the packaging: engraved glass and other personalised gifts for anniversaries, weddings, the birth of a child, a group of friends or military comrades … As in China, a bottle of wine is a prized gift.

The island also makes the most of its over-ripe fruit by distilling it, after fermentation, as 'fruit wine'. Of course the Taiwanese, who are curious travellers with a high standard of living, know the difference between these alcohols and the Western concept of wine developed from fermented grapes. The best European wines are sold in numerous stores.

MALAYSIA

BRUNEI

PHILIPPINES

MALAYSIA

SINGAPORE

Equator

Halmahera

Sumatra

Borneo

Sulawesi
(Celebes)

New
Guinea

Ceram

INDONESIA

Buru

Java

Yamdena

Sumbawa

Flores

Bali

Sumba

TIMOR-
LESTE

N

AUSTRALIA

500 km

Wines of Bali

These wines are original in three ways: for the tropical climate of the island, the grape varieties and Indonesia's Islamic tax system

In Bali, latitude 8° south, the temperature is warm all year round: 27 °C on average. The humidity varies according to the season, dry or wet, but remains high; tropical vegetation grows without a winter break. An unusual climate for the vine, which is a Mediterranean plant accustomed to a more frugal diet. Humidity causes disease (downy mildew, powdery mildew ...) but the main risk is producing an abundance of large grapes with dilute juice, without the intense flavour needed for quality winemaking.

Another feature of this island is that despite the religion being Hinduism it uses the tax system of Indonesia, the world's most populous Muslim country, and wine imports are heavily taxed. Around 1992, Ida Bagus Rai Budarsa, heir to a family of rice wine producers and holder of an invaluable distribution licence, determined to avoid these taxes on imports by making wine on the island. The Indonesian investor joined forces with French oenologist Vincent Desplat and they tried to ferment the only available grapes, the local red table variety Alphonse-Lavallée, which the local farmers grow to eat and to make offerings to their Hindu gods.

In 1994 the Hatten estate, property of Ida Bagus Rai Budarsa, launched a fresh and fruity rosé wine that was well suited to the island's spicy maritime cuisine. Every week throughout the year, the company buys grapes locally, presses them and makes wine. Trade visitors are always surprised by the small size of the press, in relation to the estate's output – 1.5 million litres per year. In temperate climates, the equipment is of course used only once a year, at the harvest season, so it has to be on a larger scale.

Once the grape harvest is over in Bali, the vines are pruned and then rebud, putting out new leaves, flowers and grapes that are harvested four months later (the year has 2.8 growing cycles). The estate now cultivates 35 hectares of a mysterious variety of white grape, Belgia Muscat, while continuing to buy red grapes from the farmers. The vines, supported by pergolas (arbours), are high yielding and the workers are simultaneously protected from the sun. They've found the perfect solution.

Twenty years of astonishingly hard work seem to have paid off: winemaking is indeed possible in the tropics. A red, two whites and two sparkling wines (traditional champagne method) complete the range. Hatten also imports frozen blocks of unfermented grape juice from Australia, including the skin and seeds – no alcohol, so no taxes – and turns them into wine in Bali under the Two Islands label.

Another unusual speciality is that Maryse La Rocque, the Quebecker who was responsible for marketing the estate, is a great fan of Pineau des Charentes, and has also launched a cuvée of the same type as this famous sweet wine: Pino de Bali, which is still in the catalogue.

Finally, an amusing paradox: this winery thrives thanks to the Islamic anti-alcohol taxation. The island's hotel chains (Hyatt, Novotel, Four Seasons, Aman ...) find it difficult to import bottles from the rest of the world to cater for their wine-loving guests, so they buy from the one and only estate on the island that uses local grapes.

Hatten doesn't export its wines. For a tasting session, you'll have to visit Bali.

ABOUT JONGLEZ PUBLISHING

It was September 1995 and Thomas Jonglez was in Peshawar, the northern Pakistani city 20 kilometres from the tribal zone he was to visit a few days later. It occurred to him that he should record the hidden aspects of his native city, Paris, which he knew so well. During his seven-month trip back home from Beijing, the countries he crossed took in Tibet (entering clandestinely, hidden under blankets in an overnight bus), Iran and Kurdistan. He never took a plane but travelled by boat, train or bus, hitch-hiking, cycling, on horseback or on foot, reaching Paris just in time to celebrate Christmas with the family.

On his return, he spent two fantastic years wandering the streets of the capital to gather material for his first 'secret guide', written with a friend. For the next seven years he worked in the steel industry until the passion for discovery overtook him. He launched Jonglez Publishing in 2003 and moved to Venice three years later.

In 2013, in search of new adventures, the family left Venice and spent six months travelling to Brazil, via North Korea, Microne-sia, the Solomon Islands, Easter Island, Peru and Bolivia. After seven years in Rio de Janeiro, he now lives in Berlin with his wife and three children.

Jonglez Publishing produces a range of titles in nine languages, released in 40 countries.

ABOUT THE AUTHOR

After training as an agricultural engineer and anthropologist, Pierrick Bourgault now travels the world to meet winemakers. His objective is to listen to their stories, to understand the diversity of their lands, grape varieties and markets. But, above all, he seeks to understand the fascinating ways plants and humans coexist, and the hazards of climate, nature and laws, particularly when they affect unusual wines – a subject that has already earned him a prize in the Wines and Territories category from the OIV (International Organisation of Vine and Wine), first prize in France's Gourmand World Cookbook Awards, and the Grand Prix du Livre Spirit in the Wines category.

Bourgault is a journalist who won the Grand Prix de l'Afja (the French association of agricultural journalists) for his media coverage in Iraq. He is the author of some 50 books on bistros, wines, photography, and life stories.

His website is at *monbar.net*

FROM THE SAME PUBLISHER

Atlas

Atlas of extreme weather
Atlas of geographical curiosities

Photo Books

Abandoned America
Abandoned Asylums
Abandoned Australia
Abandoned churches – Unclaimed places of worship
Abandoned cinemas of the world
Abandoned France
Abandoned Italy
Abandoned Japan
Abandoned Lebanon
Abandoned Spain
After the Final Curtain – The Fall of the American Movie Theater
After the Final Curtain – America's Abandoned Theaters
Baikonur – Vestiges of the Soviet Space Programme
Chernobyl's Atomic Legacy
Clickbait
Forbidden Places
Forbidden Places – Vol.2
Forbidden Places – Vol.3
Forgotten Heritage
Oblivion
Unusual wines
Venice deserted
Venice from the skies

'Soul of' Guides

Soul of Amsterdam – A guide to the 30 best experiences
Soul of Athens – A guide to 30 exceptional experiences
Soul of Barcelona – A guide to 30 exceptional experiences
Soul of Berlin – A guide to the 30 best experiences
Soul of Kyoto – A guide to 30 exceptional experiences
Soul of Lisbon – A guide to 30 exceptional experiences
Soul of Los Angeles – A guide to 30 exceptional experiences
Soul of Marrakesh – A guide to 30 exceptional experiences
Soul of New York – A guide to 30 exceptional experiencess
Soul of Rome – A guide to 30 exceptional experiencess
Soul of Tokyo – A guide to 30 exceptional experiences
Soul of Venice – A guide to 30 exceptional experiences

'Secret' Guides

Secret Amsterdam
Secret Bali
Secret Bangkok
Secret Barcelona
Secret Belfast
Secret Berlin
Secret Brighton – An unusual guide
Secret Brooklyn
Secret Brussels
Secret Buenos Aires
Secret Campania
Secret Cape Town
Secret Copenhagen
Secret Dublin – An unusual guide
Secret Edinburgh – An unusual guide
Secret Florence
Secret French Riviera
Secret Geneva
Secret Glasgow
Secret Granada
Secret Helsinki
Secret Istanbul
Secret Johannesburg
Secret Lisbon
Secret Liverpool – An unusual guide
Secret London – An unusual guide
Secret London – Unusual bars & restaurants
Secret Los Angeles
Secret Madrid
Secret Mexico City

Secret Milan
Secret Montreal - An unusual guide
Secret Naples
Secret New Orleans
Secret New York – An unusual guide
Secret New York – Curious activities
Secret New York – Hidden bars & restaurants
Secret Paris
Secret Prague
Secret Provence
Secret Rio
Secret Rome
Secret Seville
Secret Singapore
Secret Sussex – An unusual guide
Secret Tokyo
Secret Tuscany
Secret Venice
Secret Vienna
Secret York – An unusual guide

Secret Washington D.C.
Secret York - An unusual guide

Follow us on Facebook, Instagram and Twitter

Cartography: **Cyrille Suss** – Translation: **Caroline Lawrence and Olivia Fuller** –
Layout: **Emmanuelle Willard Toulemonde** – Copy-Editing: **Jana Gough and Lee Dickinson** –
Proofreading: **Kimberly Bess** – Publishing: **Clémence Mathé**

Cover: *Treille*, **Friedrich Kersting (1815) – Kunst Museum Düsseldorf**

© JONGLEZ 2023

Registration of copyright: September 2023 – Edition: 01

ISBN: 978-2-36195-583-0

Printed in Slovakia by Polygraf